DOUBLE TAXATION TREATIES BETWEEN INDUSTRIALISED AND DEVELOPING COUNTRIES; OECD AND UN MODELS, A COMPARISON

INTERNATIONAL FISCAL ASSOCIATION

Proceedings of a Seminar held in Stockholm in 1990 during the 44th Congress of the International Fiscal Association

Vol. 15

KLUWER LAW AND TAXATION PUBLISHERS
DEVENTER · BOSTON

Kluwer Law and Taxation Publishers
P.O. Box 23 Tel. : 31-5700-47261
7400 GA Deventer Telex : 49295
The Netherlands Fax : 31-5700-22244

Library of Congress Cataloging-in-Publication Data

Double taxation treaties between industrial and developing countries:
OECD and UN models, a comparison: proceedings of a seminar held in Stockholm in 1990 during the 44th Congress of the International Fiscal Association / International Fiscal Association.
p. cm. -- (IFA congress seminar series: V. 15)
ISBN 9065446109
1. Taxation, Double -- Treaties -- Congresses. I. International Fiscal Association. II. International Fiscal Association. Congress (44th: 1990: Stockholm, Sweden) III. Series: IFA congress seminar series: 15.
K4474.61990
341.4'844'026--dc20 91-45483
CIP

ISBN 90 6544 610 9

DOUBLE TAXATION TREATIES BETWEEN INDUSTRIALISED AND DEVELOPING COUNTRIES; OECD AND UN MODELS, A COMPARISON

Proceedings of a Seminar held in Stockholm in 1990 during the 44th Congress of the International Fiscal Association*

Chairman of the Seminar
L. Mutén (Sweden)
Professor of International Tax Law at the Stockholm School of Economics.
Formerly: Senior Advisor Fiscal Affairs Department, International Monetary Fund, Washington

Panelists:
Dr. A.H. Figueroa (Argentina)
National Director of Taxes, Subsecretariat of Public Finance, Ministry of Economic Affairs, Buenos Aires

J.F. Court (France)
General Director Europar. Formerly: international tax division chief of France

O.P. Vaish (India)
Senior Advocate, Vaish Associates, Inc.

M. Collins (United Kingdom)
Formerly: Assistant Secretary of the UK Board of Inland Revenue

M.S. Feinberg (USA)
Department of the Treasury, Washington

**The views expressed are those of the authors and not necessarily those of the International Fiscal Association*

IFA CONGRESS SEMINAR SERIES*

1. Work in Intergovernmental Organizations on Transnational Companies (Congress 1976)

2. The Revised OECD Model Double Taxation Convention on Income and Capital (Congress 1977)

3. Fiscal Policy and Tax Structures in the Pacific Region (Congress 1978)

4. UN Draft Model Taxation Convention (Congress 1979)

5. Recourse to Tax Havens - Use and Abuse (Congress 1980)

6. Taxation of the Income Arising from the International Seabed (Congress 1981)

7. Imputation Systems - Objectives and Consequences (Congress 1982)

8. Tax Policy towards the National Heritage (Congress 1983)

9. Adjustments for Tax Purposes in Highly Inflationary Economies (Congress 1984)

10. International Tax Problems of Charities and other Private Institutions with similar Tax Treatment (Congress 1985)

11a. Taxation of domestic shareholders on undistributed income of foreign corporate affiliates: objectives, techniques and consequences (Congress 1986)

11b. International Tax Treatment of Common Law Trusts (Congress 1986)

12. Taxation and Human Rights (Congress 1987)

13a. Data Processing in Taxation (Congress 1988)

* Available from Kluwer Law and Taxation Publishers
P.O. Box 23
7400 GA Deventer, The Netherlands
(tel.:+31 5700 47261 - fax +31 5700 22244)

13b. Tax Consequences of Pension Provision for the Internationally Transferred Employee (Congress 1988)

14a. International Taxation of Services (Congress 1989)

14b. Tax Treaties and Domestic Legislation (Congress 1989)

15. 'Double Taxation Treaties between Industrialised and Developing Countries; OECD and UN Models, a Comparison' (Congress 1990)

Table of Contents

I. *Proceedings of the Seminar*

Double taxation conventions between industrialised and developing countries
L. Mutén (Sweden) ... 3

Comprehensive tax treaties
A.H. Figueroa (Argentina) ... 9

Some reflections on the experience of the UN Model in tax treaties between developed and developing countries.
J.F. Court (France) ... 15

Double tax conventions between industrialised and developing countries: India's experience
O.P. Vaish (India) ... 21

Brief survey of the development and main features of the United Kingdom's double taxation agreements with developing countries
M. Collins (United Kingdom) ... 27

United States views on selected aspects of developing country tax treaty issues
M.S. Feinberg (USA) ... 39

II. *Summary of Proceedings*

Dr. J.B. Bracewell-Milnes (United Kingdom) ... 49

I. PROCEEDINGS OF THE SEMINAR

DOUBLE TAXATION CONVENTIONS BETWEEN INDUSTRIALISED AND DEVELOPING COUNTRIES

L. Mutén (Sweden)

This seminar has been arranged to take stock of developments following the 1980 publication of the UN model tax convention. Papers have been presented by five panel members, two from developing countries, Argentina and India, three from industrial countries, France, UK, and USA. These contributions offer an excellent basis for our discussion.

Initially, it should be noted that the UN model came about in recognition of the fact that the OECD model, basically built on the assumption of reciprocity in the relations between treaty countries, is not quite appropriate for treaty relationships where no reciprocity exists. One might add that for many developing countries, international considerations relate to a relatively important part of the tax base, foreign ownership being important in the modern sector of the economy, expatriates being employed to a significant extent, services and know-how being procured from foreign suppliers, and substantial interest and royalty payments being made to recipients abroad. Hence, tax concessions offered may often imply that significant revenue amounts are forgone. Therefore, many issues that in the OECD context could be solved on the basis of simplicity and practicability, would be seen in a different light in the treaty relationship between industrial and developing countries. The solution would often be of real importance to the budget of the developing country involved.

The UN model, moreover, is the product of a group of experts not officially representing their governments, nor representing all the developing or industrial countries whose interests were at stake in the discussions. The importance of the issues and the limited mandate of the experts producing the model obviously had to result in a model convention of a kind different from the OECD model, leaving more to negotiation in each particular case.

Accordingly, while we must all recognize the rationale for the UN model, we must also understand the reason why it had to differ from the OECD model. It is also quite clear that the UN model, while certainly representing a most impressive effort to come to terms with the many issues involved, is still not seen by all as the final solution to all of them.

We are, in that respect, lucky to have Mr. Figueroa's candid paper that sets out quite clearly the reasoning of those who feel that the developing country representatives were too forthcoming in the search for a compromise within the group of experts, and who see a general source country rule as the only viable solution to the double taxation problem.

Perhaps the more positive evaluation of the UN model on the side of the discussants from industrial countries could be interpreted as a tacit admission that the UN model is still too close to the OECD model to be regarded as a real compromise. Another, probably more realistic way of seeing the issue is that the relatively much smaller revenue significance of the issues makes for a more detached attitude on the side of these representatives.

Panel members were invited to deal with the whole range of issues; space restrictions have made for concentration on relatively few, and this is probably what should be expected. Here, I should like to concentrate the matter even further, bringing up just a few of the issues dealt with by most or all discussants.

1. Do we need Treaties?

The panel votes four to one on the issue whether there should be double tax treaties between industrial and developing countries, Mr. Figueroa being against, Mr. Collins delivering the most eloquent argument in defense. The majority vote in a small panel is, of course, not the answer. Nor can we draw any firm conclusions from the fact that Mr. Vaish from India, a country playing a leading role in the development of tax treaties not just of the type we talk about here, but in the equally interesting South-South context, has come out firmly in stating that treaties between industrial and developing countries are in their mutual interest. What the panel has to say is therefore rather nuanced:

First of all, taxes are not an all-important issue overriding all others. If investment in a non-treaty country is sufficiently attractive, investors will come, regardless of how tough the tax climate and how incomplete the tax treaty network. The reciprocal statement also holds: if circumstances are sufficiently unattractive in non-tax respects, no tax relief and no tax treaty can bring in the unwilling investors.

Second, we need to answer the question '*cui bono?*', in other words who gets the relief? If contracts - be they on credits, leasing, royalties, or even employment - are negotiated on the basis of net of tax payments, it can be argued that it is the payor rather than the recipient of the income who is the one interested in lower tax. If government finds that the use of foreign production factors should be penalized to make domestic alternatives relatively more attractive, there is not very much interest on either side in tax reliefs or treaty provisions in general. On the other hand, if it is felt that double taxation has a stifling effect on economic activities, it can be seen as an advantage, if tax reliefs tend to benefit the domestic payors without very much affecting the net payments to recipients abroad. Perhaps we need some qualifications to our possibly too simplistic ideas on who makes consessions and who picks up the benefits.

Third, treaties have a signal effect, in two respects. One is that a country does not make tax treaties if it aims at establishing itself as a tax haven; making treaties may even offer a certain assurance against being blacklisted in countries apprehensive about international tax avoidance and evasion. The other signal effect is to investors and other potential business partners. The willingness of a country to enter tax treaties indicates to these groups that the country wants to accommodate them in offering an acceptable economic climate including a reasonable degree of stability in tax matters. While the incentive effect of this might be limited, it certainly cannot hurt.

Fourth, tax treaties can be a necessary condition for making tax concessions effective. This aspect leads us into the tax sparing issue.

2. Tax-sparing

The tax-sparing issue has been discussed many times before at IFA congresses. The basic conflict is unresolved. On the one hand, host countries resent the idea of incentives offered being rendered ineffective by residence countries refusing credit for tax not effectively paid. On the other hand, a residence country may - at least in principle - adhere to the idea of taxation being imposed generally without other exceptions than those provided by its own legalisation. To an extent, this conflict has been deepened, in as much as many industrial countries have reduced or abolished their tax incentive programs in favor of lower general rates. The somewhat patronizing argument against tax sparing, namely, that tax incentives are not actually in the best interest of the countries offering them, has gained strength through this development, although it is difficult to discern a corresponding general trend in developing countries in favor of liquidating their incentive programs.

To some extent, the conflict has calmed down as the result of a number of developments. First among those may well be the readiness of a great number of important capital-exporting countries to agree to tax sparing provisions in their treaties, to the extent they do not go even further by exempting the income categories at issue. Second, the restrictions on the foreign tax credit imposed both by lowered domestic tax rates and by detailed anti-abuse provisions, have led to a situation in which a great number of investors find themselves in an excess credit position. This has the consequence for investors that they may themselves enjoy their tax reliefs rather than just seeing them reduce their foreign tax credit. Third, many capital-importing countries have realized that they might benefit most from incentives offered with respect to retained profits rather than repatriated ones. With respect to the former, as long as tax deferral is the rule, the tax-sparing issue will not come up.

This last point brings us to another matter of importance in the tax-sparing context, namely, the importance of tax deferral. Capital-exporting countries could, for reasons of domestic tax equity, or for whatever other reason, abolish the prevailing rule deferring shareholders' tax on foreign company profits until such profits are distributed. In that case, the tax-sparing issue would again come to the forefront. Obviously, tax deferral is not a rule without exceptions; as long as the exceptions just refer to income of the 'Subpart F' type, however, the issue of tax-sparing is not a very burning one in that context.

On all these points, I feel that Mr. Feinberg's contribution offers a fair and enlightening view of the special position of the United States.

3. Permanent Establishment

The definition of permanent establishment (Art. 5) is one of the points where the UN model and the OECD model differ most. Some critics of the UN model even felt that adopting the concept represented an original sin of the *ad hoc* group. Reference was made to the Cartagena model, in which the Andean Pact states agreed to a model not using the concept at all. Yet, the definition of what the Cartagena model understands under doing business in a country is strikingly similar to the OECD model, and even more to the UN model.

It seems quite clear that there are conflicting interests at stake here, not just between the countries negotiating a tax treaty, but on each side of the negotiating table. The host country has a material interest in as broad a tax base as possible, be it to collect tax, be it to give effect to incentive schemes. The same host country also has an interest in paving the road for prospective investors by offering a friendly business climate. Such a climate is not brought about by making every business visitor, however temporary and casual, a client of the tax administration. Hence some moderation in the expansion of the permanent establishment concept may be seen as in the interest of the host country as well as in the interest of the country of domicile.

As has been interestingly spelled out in Mr. Feinberg's paper, the domicile country, while basically interested in a restrictive formulation of the permanent establishment definition, may still prefer a wide definition in cases such as leasing, where the inclusion of a certain activity implies the taxation of net income as opposed to the gross income taxation applicable in the case of the activity falling outside the definition. In this respect, it is interesting to note Mr. Vaish's warm endorsement of gross income taxes even in cases where the permanent establishment rule would apply.

Another aspect of the permanent establishment concept is the technical development that makes it possible to circumvent the definition while maintaining the business activity. In a world where we are seriously discussing whether we need to demand our office staff to go to work or whether we could let them stay at home with a computer terminal, we should not be surprised at the amount of business that can be dealt with at a distance with the help of computer networks and fax machines. In light of Mr. Vaish's report, it is conceivable that those trying to keep outside the definition of permanent establishment will instead find themselves hit by gross taxation, the alternative for them being local incorporation. If it were generally felt that the technical opportunities of escaping the permanent establishment status need to be curtailed by this array of rules, one might pose the question what purpose would still be served by the permanent establishment rule.

4. Transfer Pricing

It is interesting to note that our discussion has not indicated any new tendencies with respect to the transfer pricing provisions. Quite clearly, we are heading for trouble in this area, mainly as a result of more attention being paid to it and more administrative resources being mobilized in a growing number of important industrial countries. For the developing countries, it is difficult to answer up to this tendency. Transfer pricing is a difficult subject for any tax administration, and in developing countries, the tax administrations rarely find themselves able to give the matter the attention needed to counter the findings of more resourceful administrations in industrial countries.

The purpose of a double tax convention is not fulfilled, if one country makes adjustment of transfer prices implying a higher profit taxable in that country, whereas the other country refuses to make the reciprocal adjustment. On the other hand, neither the OECD nor the UN model makes it an unconditional obligation of the other state to make a reciprocal adjustment. An amicable solution under the mutual agreement procedure prescribed in Art. 25 is obviously the outcome envisaged by the expert group. Nevertheless, the temptation may be strong to make experiments with unitary apportionment or resort to minimum assessments.

Neither solution is promising. Unitary apportionment is if possible an even more difficult method for developing countries than for industrial countries. Quite apart from the obvious complication of enforcing a claim on international groups to produce worldwide returns translated into the currency and set up in accordance with the tax law of each country in which the group may have a permanent establishment it is also difficult to see any equity to the developing countries in the apportionment keys normally discussed.

Turnover normally excludes intra-group transactions, and, if it does not, raises the usual transfer pricing problem the apportionment rule was supposed to avoid. Payroll is low in low-wage countries, and compensation to expatriate staff is often paid elsewhere to avoid excessive taxes in poor host countries. Capital assets are hard to value and plant is normally much better equipped and much more expensive in the industrial base countries than in the poor host countries.

There remains the minimum assessment method, a necessary evil, perhaps, in particular in countries where tax compliance is poor and where it is felt that the need for the Treasury to have a stable flow of revenue is even greater than for enterprises to get a break in loss years. The application of a minimum assessment rule, normally related to real or estimated turnover, is not without problems, either. The foreign tax credit rules of other countries may deem a minimum tax to be a turnover tax, provided the main tax is not a real income tax against which the turnover related minimum tax is normally credited; if the minimum tax is too high, so as to make it the normal tax rather than the exception, the credit is in earnest jeopardy.

If instead of as a minimum tax, the gross income tax is imposed as the only and final tax, say, on non-residents in general, say, on certain types of business, the foreign tax credit in the home countries is even more at risk, however practical the solution might seem and however desirable, as Mr. Vaish indicates, for non-resident taxpayers seeking stability and certainty in their relationship with the tax authorities.

6. Exchange of Information

This brings us to the important issue of cooperation. As a matter of fact, we have seen in recent years a tendency among tax administrators to attach their main attention to that part of the treaties, to the extent of making treaties on exchange of information only, dropping the double taxation provisions.

Interestingly, Mr. Court in his paper mentions the French experience of exchange of information sometimes working even better in the relationship with developing countries than with certain European Community countries. The explanation lies at hand in the common legal tradition and the common language in the French community of countries, yet, it is encouraging in a general perspective. Of course, some of us might feel that cooperation between tax authorities is a matter of little interest or even of negative interest to the taxpaying community. In contrast, it can well be argued that it is not in the interest of the taxpaying community to see the cooperation between tax authorities frustrated. Countries feeling that they are facing an insurmountable task in coping with transnational enterprises will much more likely resort to undesirable, rough-and-ready methods than they would, if they felt that they could rely on mutual cooperation with other tax authorities to make the tax system work.

COMPREHENSIVE TAX TREATIES

A.H. Figueroa (Argentina)

I. Tax Treaties between developing Countries and industrialised Countries - are they an apparent or a real Need?

Empirical evidence shows that comprensive tax treaties are not, as was generally supposed, an essential instrument for promoting and intensifying the flow of investments towards countries that are relatively less developed economically. There are numerous examples in support of this statement, significant investments having been carried out without the backing of any tax treaty whatsoever. This can be seen as proving that the tax factor, even though admittedly important, does not generally play a decisive part among the factors that determine external investment decisions.

Historical development tells us that during the 60's, it was generally understood that treaties might constitute an adequate instrument to influence the flow of external investments to the poorest countries. However, despite the many agreements that were signed, mainly at the initiative of the industrialised countries, developing countries soon realized that the stipulations imposed on them in negotiations, equivalent to those being used in the industrial countries' agreements among themselves, did not sufficiently take regard to the legitimate fiscal interests of the developing countries. This was not only because many of these countries allocate to themselves the power to tax strictly on the basis of the principle of territoriality of the source, and in consequence do not tax income elements derived from external sources. It was also because the flows of investments and income between the two types of countries are typically, indeed almost always, one-way flows. That is to say, although developing countries adopted the principle of taxing worldwide income, they had, as typical source countries, only the sacrifices arising from the signing of conventions, without deriving any real compensation for these sacrifices from the corresponding sacrifices imposed, in form rather than in reality, on the other contracting state. In other words, the developing countries became aware that in signing an agreement with a developed country, what they in fact were negotiating away was the right to tax income generated under their jurisdiction by investments undertaken by developed countries.

Thus, to attract external investment, new negotiations were carried on based on the idea of giving up conventional neutrality. In its place, a combination was sought, on the one hand, of fiscal sacrifices in the form of special fiscal promotion measures - exemptions from tax or reduction of the effective rates - on the other hand of tax relief in the other contracting state. Such relief could consist of an outright exemption from tax of income derived from the developing country, or of tax sparing or matching credit, normally provided for under special clauses in the double tax conventions.

If the matter is analyzed under the aspect of benefits derived from the signing of comprehensive tax agreements, the governments or tax authorities of the capital exporting countries are the ones who obtain the real advantages from such treaties. Among the advantages it is worth highlighting such features as that their right to levy taxes is given priority, that they retain the exclusive right to tax certain business benefits, that there is a reduction or elimination of taxes at source for other types of income, and that the capital-exporting countries are able to obtain information providing enhanced control over their taxpayers. Fundamentally, the treaties respond to the pressures of investors to mitigate their total tax burden, avoid their exposure to discriminatory treatment, and resolve potential conflicts by means of agreed procedures.

As regards the investors, the treaties being analyzed also carry various advantages in addition to those mentioned in the previous paragraph. Thus, they may be able to transfer certain expenses that can be included in transfer prices set and explicitly or implicitly make them deductible twice over. The treaties also provide for separate accounting rather than a unitary apportionment, and this contributes to flexible tax planning, including remuneration for financial and technological services. Investors are also at times offered an additional benefit in the form of tax sparing, and moreover they enjoy lower withholding tax rates. In all, they achieve a framework of tax rules that attenuates the difficulties that would probably derive from future recurrent tax law changes, such as usually take place in developing countries.

Nevertheless, considering the fact that the tax factor does not constitute an element entering into the decision to invest, the tax treaties do not take on the relevance that is usually attributed to them. That is why they do not in any way appear to constitute a necessary prerequisite to attract foreign capital. Besides, it would perhaps be more logical to fit them into a set of dual aspirations, held by the tax authority of the investor's domicile country and by the investor himself. The former has as its objective to satisfy the claim for horizontal equity among taxpayers with the least possible sacrifice of revenue. The latter wants to maximize his profit and minimize his risk. Both aspirations appear both valid and legitimate, even though their satisfaction may not be a necessary condition for the flow of investments to come about. In fact, the true problem consists in the adoption of subject-oriented jurisdictional principles - domicile or residence - which implies subjecting to tax the worldwide income in the country receiving the profit, beyond the taxation that is the legitimate right of the source country.

To conclude, capital-exporting countries seem to be both the victims and the victimizers of the jurisdictional principle - domicile, residence, or even citizenship - that they have adopted. They are the victims of constant pressure from their own taxpayers to ensure that the level of the tax burden does not exceed the level laid down under their own domestic law. On the other hand, however, they are victimizers when they harm the interests of developing countries by insisting on leveling the total tax burden by imposing this kind of model conventions that curb legitimate fiscal resources of poorer countries under the pretext of facilitating the establishment of an instrument to encourage investment flows to these countries. If we examine the situation facing taxpayers domiciled or resident in developing countries, regardless of the jurisdictional principle adopted by these countries in their national legislation - source, domicile, or residence - these taxpayers do not normally suffer any negative effects of international double taxation. The reason is, of course, that they do not receive income from external sources, with the exception of those in the upper income brackets, who have significant financial investments (capital flight), but their investments are mainly in certain developed countries that set up genuine barriers for the tax authorities in the relatively less developed countries.

Besides, the so-called favorable climate for investment does constitute the most pertinent aspect in deciding where to establish capital investments. It is well known that in this climate a number of aspects of diverse nature that are not connected with taxation come to the fore, such as security and stability as well as a number of conditions of an economic nature. When those conditions are not present, the signing of tax treaties does not seem advisable, since this will always entail waiving the right to tax resources, whereas there will not be a proper corrective entry of advantages to the country. Nevertheless, there is admittedly a case for a developing country to pay the price entailed in the signing of a tax treaty, adopting one of the models suggested by industrialised countries. That is when it can be done within the framework of a global agreement or set of agreements, pre-existing or concurrent, that entail a certain and effective economic, commercial, and financial support. Otherwise, the signing of such tax agreements imply a useless fiscal sacrifice.

II. The OECD and UN Models

The 1963 OECD model (the blue book), as amended in 1977, is the embodiment of a typical conventional structure providing economically relatively more developed countries with the opportunity of having an instrument available for facilitating negotiations with other such countries. The model treaty constitutes a bilateral tax framework oriented towards avoiding the interference of fiscal factors in the decisions and preferences of the parties involved in economic activities in two of those states.

Member countries have also used this model to enter into agreements with non-industralised countries. They have encouraged these countries to negotiate with the pretense that such a model represented a proper instrument for promoting and intensifying the flow of investments towards those countries. The dual purpose attributed to the model, one of neutrality intended in some relations, one of non-neutral promotion of investments in another, could not stand up to any reasonably serious analysis. Therefore, the Secretary General of the United Nations, following a decision of its Economic and Social Council, convoked a Group of Experts from both types of countries in 1967, charging them with the task of drawing up a model that, based on the characteristics assumed to apply to the relationship between developing countries and industrialised countries, would constitute a tool for contributing to the flow of investments towards the former group of countries.

After twelve years, in 1979, the *ad hoc* group of experts approved a model that is known as the United Nations model (the yellow book). Notwithstanding the different color of its cover, this model shows definite and clear similarities with the OECD model. In spite of the claims made by the developing countries, and the fact that the UN model at certain points offers some limited modifications of the OECD model aimed at better fitting the relationship between industrialised and developing countries, the model does not fulfill the objectives set by the Secretary General when convoking the experts representing both groups of countries, and certainly not the requirements of the developing countries. At this first stage, the yellow book is a faithful reflexion of the predominant position of the industrialised countries that apart from differences at certain points show a homogenous substantial position both with respect to the general environment and the specific purposes of the tax treaties. In contrast, the group of developing countries did not show the same clear harmony of purpose, and this because of different reasons, such as cultural dependence on other countries and the general diversity within the group. As a logical consequence of the approval of an inadequate model, we find that the conflict between the two groups of countries remains unresolved. The developing countries consider that the model does not satisfy their just and valid claims with respect to the preservation of their right to exercise their power to tax. Meanwhile, some industrialised countries consider the model imprecise and too generous. That the latter attitude can be taken shows how restrictive the criteria are that guide the competent authorities of those countries. This consideration raises important doubts with respect to the real intentions of developed countries in the context of promoting investment in countries that are economically relatively less developed.

III. Is an alternative Solution possible?

The OECD model is not suited to the objectives pursued by the developing countries. The UN model does not meet them because it is undeniably based on the OECD model, while at the same time failing to fully satisfy the industrialised countries, although they admit the validity of some particular clauses. In view of these facts, it must be admitted that it seems gradually to become ever more improbable that agreements will be reached between countries belonging to these different groups. Hence, it will be necessary to resolve double taxation problems affecting taxpayers of industrialised countries receiving foreign source income from developing countries, mainly by unilateral remedies or measures contained in the laws of their countries of residence.

In different international forums, representatives of the private sector in the industrialised countries have pointed out that from their vantage point, they would prefer to be subject solely to taxation in the source country, rather than being subject to taxes in both jurisdictions involved. In this connection, the 38th IFA congress held in Buenos Aires in 1984 came out in favor of the exclusive right of the source country to levy taxes, both because this would offer a greater measure of respect for the tax sovereignty of the nations and because it would be away with the distortions of competition in the country where the investment is made and thus not interfere with the free flow of investments. If their exclusive right to tax were taken as a starting point, it is possible that the developing countries would show more inclination towards solving the tax problems of the foreign investors. They might then be ready to agree to some limitation of the withholding tax rates, to some non-discrimination clauses, and to other measures aimed at offering clear signals to their potential investors as regards the construction of a reasonable and stable tax framework.

Nevertheless, it is not deemed probable that the alternative here suggested will be accepted by the governments of the industrialised countries, even though it may be favorably evaluated by their taxpayers, who are the beneficiaries of foreign source income. The conceptions prevailing at the government level in industrial countries are opposed to a change such as that suggested here. That is why it is considered extremely difficult to achieve any quick progress in changing the rules of the game that these countries have laid down. For this reason, it is also unlikely that the perspective of the capital importing countries will include any good reasons for increasing the bilateral negotiating activity. As time goes by, these countries assign ever less importance to the signing of comprehensive tax agreements.

SOME REFLECTIONS ON THE EXPERIENCE OF THE UN MODEL IN TAX TREATIES BETWEEN DEVELOPED AND DEVELOPING COUNTRIES

J.F. Court (France)

The OECD tax treaty is the result of quite a long history. The consideration of international tax problems began in the 1920's. The development of international economic relations after World War Two gave these reflections new impetus. This movement ended up in the publication of the OECD model in 1963, which was later revised in 1977. This proposed model is based mostly on European tax systems, defined between the two World Wars. It was issued in the sixties, that is at the end of an unprecedented period of reconstruction and growth of market economies (United States and European, as well as Japanese) and before the crisis of the seventies.

After 1960, as new independent countries emerged on the international scene, emphasis was put on development problems. The United Nations took up a growing role, especially in this area of economic development. Hence it embarked on the task of trying to define a framework for the tax relations between developed and less developed countries. A group of experts was organized which decided to try to adapt the OECD model to this specific relationship.

From the beginning, this has been a touchy task given the sensitivity of the issue in less developed countries. It is argued that they did not form a united front, which is true, if only because of widely different economic situations. One does not see any valid reason why they should have presented a united front: the experts were named on a personal basis, and the issue being, after all, not one of confrontation! Moreover, even if their experts were divided, that may also be said of experts from developed countries. The views of the Swiss, the French and the American experts were most certainly different! This would be, in the opinion of this writer, rather a positive point in favor of the UN model!

Nevertheless, this work eventually ended up in the publication of the UN model, the 'yellow book', which, like it or not, has had a lot of influence on the various negotiations which have taken place between developed and developing countries during this period. It has thus played a very important role, and it is indeed interesting, given the criticism it encounters, to try to fairly assess its role.

Criticism has been based on several issues:

-the technical issue of adapting a treaty designed for relations between developed countries to make it a tool for developing countries;

-the fact that tax aspects are not paramount in the decisions of investment;

-hence, tax treaties not being that useful to begin with and the UN model not being adapted to the desires of non developed countries, treaty negotiations and the UN model should be dropped altogether.

It is interesting to review these criticisms in light of recent world changes in terms of economic development and/or political evolution.

Technically, this writer does not think that the UN model is not adapted to developing countries but rather that the models themselves (including the OECD one) may not always be adapted to modern transactions. If the relative importance of the tax element appears to be a fact, the conclusion that the UN model is useless is not shared at all by this writer. To the contrary.

1. Technical Aspects

Before going to more general comments, it seems useful to stress that the UN model (as well as in fact the OECD model) is technically quite adapted to relations between developed and developing countries.

First of all, the approach it takes, on the same lines as the OECD model, is the approach taken the world over when international tax problems are discussed. The terms, definitions, analyses and interactions of concepts are common, even if the provisions in each individual case may vary widely. The common body is in itself an important aspect. As 'an old tax is a good tax' as the common saying goes, stressing the importance of acceptance and understanding, it can be said of the UN model that 'a generally accepted framework is a good framework'.

Stemming from the schedular tax systems of Europe well known in many developing countries, it gives a frame which is neither too global (as it might have been, had it been designed only in the light of the global tax systems applied in Anglo-Saxon countries), nor rendered too complex by endless detailed provisions. It also allows quite a degree of flexibility and adaptation in its structure, while at the same time staying in a quite unified international framework, rendering tax analysis easier.

Proof of this resilience of the model structure is the fact that many treaties have been negotiated between industrial and developing countries and that they appear widely to use this framework, even though there are, of course, many differences between them.

Although I think that the structure of the OECD model is not necessarily well adapted to present economic relations and should be reviewed (for example with a new emphasis on service transactions, transfers of technology, information, communication and cultural activities, etc. ...), this is the main reason why one should be cautious with respect to proposals for overhauling the system.

At this point, this writer would like to address *some technical issues* concerning the application of tax treaties between developed and developing countries and the use of the UN model, in light of the French experience:

- among the *specific provisions proposed by the UN model,* those relating to the permanent establishment, to sales income, to service transactions and to complex contracts have been widely used and refined. It is clear that for countries depending on foreign technology, this is a very important borderline issue. The relevant provisions have often been supplemented with specific provisions aimed at apportioning income or expenses with a view to avoid implementation problems (for exemple in the relations between France and Morocco). In these aspects, the UN model has shown its adaptability (often embodied in long protocols to the treaty). Along the same line, in various French tax treaties, one can point out specific provisions, inspired by the UN approach and aimed at tackling allocation and transfer pricing problems by simple, easily applicable, *forfait* rules. Altogether, this experience, despite problems here and there, is quite satisfactory.
- *the tax sparing issue* is more complex. Tax sparing is widely used in French tax treaties and the experience is rather positive. However, given the recent decrease in the French corporate tax rate and the level of taxation in source countries, even with tax sparing provisions, tax sparing clauses are often too powerful and thus give rise to technical difficulties or even to quasi-evasion schemes. A fair assessment is that tax sparing provisions are useful but should not be overplayed. In particular, the national rates which are often based on gross income, should be kept in a reasonable range.
- *exchange of information and competent authority procedures* are more difficult to assess. Exchange of information may work quite well between a developed and a developing country and France has some good experience in this respect. But confidence in the use of information, the quality of the administration and of taxpayer protection are of paramount importance. Ironically, France has competent authority procedure experience with some developing countries of a better quality than it has experienced with some EEC member countries! Here again, historical links, personal relationships and overall confidence are very important.

2. The relative Importance of the Tax Element in international Decisions

The case is often made that tax aspects play a relatively modest role in international relations, especially in decisions concerning capital flows or foreign investments.

It has been clear for a long time that the quality of the global environment is of utmost importance. Political stability, the capacity to develop and properly manage the necessary infrastructure, the capacity of self-government (including proper judicial protections and civil liberties), the capacity to curb corruption and the capacity to adapt the country to a market economy (playing up its strengths, smoothly downplaying its weaknesses) are key factors. More important - and this is to some extent a cultural question - the capacity of the country's elite to have faith in itself and in its country instead of channeling resources into tax havens is the driving force of most economic development. It is often true that such resources are too freely provided by shortsighted financial institutions in developed countries, playing 'pousse-au-crime'.

This delicate balance, difficult to attain (even in developed countries!), is the main reason for development. In this respect, it is true that the tax aspect is a secondary issue.

The situation today in developing countries is an example of this: the development of South East Asian countries bears testimony to the role of governing capacity, hard work and the importance of having faith. The problems faced by Africa or South America offer witness to the contrary. Argentina, endowed with vast resources and an educated population, was in 1939 the 8th world power, in 1946 the 6th, at a time when Korea was still virtually in the middle ages and largely unheard of. Aside from any international polemic, have not the Argentinians and the Koreans had something to do with the situation today?

As a result of this global analysis, the case is made that Double Taxation Agreements are useless. It is said that as the UN model is perceived as too biased towards the interests of developed countries, it should be discarded.

But, even if it is not a major element, I think that the tax aspect is important and should be taken into account by the developed and developing countries. And for that the UN model is still a useful tool.

3. Good Use of the UN Model

Even if the attractiveness of a given country to foreign investors is based on general features, the decision to invest and the subsequent management of the investment will heavily take into account financial aspects. Along with legal protection of the investment, exchange control regulations, labor or commercial laws, taxation will then be a very important factor.

Of course, most important will generally be the host country tax system in general rather than the specific provisions of a tax treaty, because in most cases there will be exposure to local taxation. Hence, the rules, the tax rates, but also the fairness of the administration, the absence of corruption, etc. will be taken into account by the decision makers. But, once the host country situation is viewed as satisfactory, given the opportunity the market represents, then the international issues will come into play with force. First, for example at the pre-investment stage: study of an operation, opening of a liaison bureau. And then in the operation itself: profit taxation and transfer of after-tax profits, treatment of dividends, royalties, interest, etc.

In this view, the tax treaty (as well as other treaties such as investment protection treaties) is one important element of the overall climate. Surely, the importance of a particular provision should not be overplayed (except if there is a very specific situation). Both sides should show some flexibility in this respect. In its treaties, France has shown a good amount of flexibility regarding the permanent establishement principe, the withholding taxes, and the matching credits.

Some basic principles should be kept in mind:

- concerning international money management, it is a fact that the taxation is small or nil, the example being set by developed countries, with the US in the first place. Therefore, countries (in their treaties, as well as in their domestic law) must strike a delicate balance between the necessities of international financing and those of internal tax equity;

- the fine tuning of a tax rate is of less importance to an enterprise than the way the tax rules are applied: when there are arbitrary decisions, corruption, even physical threats to employees for tax reasons, as I have seen in extreme cases, a low tax rate or an exemption does not mean much. When there is a market and a fair tax to be paid on a profit which may then be freely transferred, there is no excuse not to pay...

And, again, facts are quite clear: it is not just by happenstance that in the relationships between developed and developing countries one finds that those developing countries which enjoy the highest degree of growth are also those whose treaties are the closest to the OECD or UN models. The experiences of countries like Singapore, Thailand, Korea and Indonesia are quite illustrative.

In conclusion, it can be said that tax treaties are a useful tool, but only as a part of a general context favorable to development. Their role should neither be overestimated, nor underestimated.

At that level, having taken into account the relative importance of what is at stake, I think that the work that has been done by the UN group resulting in the UN model, represents a significant achievement nobody has to be ashamed of. And a strong case can be made, in today's rapidly changing world, for pursuing this work in good faith at least among nations desiring to achieve or help achieve harmonious development.

DOUBLE TAX CONVENTIONS BETWEEN INDUSTRIALISED AND DEVELOPING COUNTRIES: INDIA'S EXPERIENCE

O.P. Vaish (India)

My first IFA Congress was at Stockholm in 1967. The Subject II at that Congress was 'Harmonization of the concept of permanent establishment in double tax conventions'. Harmonization was then mainly discussed in the context of conventions between industrialised countries. I recall that, in the draft resolution on the subject, it was recommended that the view point of the developing countries on the subject should be accommodated. I had taken exception to the word 'accommodated'. The bilateral tax conventions between industrialised and developing countries are of mutual advantage and, therefore, the word 'accommodated' was not appropriate. I was happy that the reservation expressed by me was appreciated, especially by members of The Netherlands Branch of IFA, and the draft was suitably modified.

1. The very next year the United Nations set up the *ad hoc* group of experts on tax treaties between developed and developing countries. The UN Model Convention was published in 1980. As on date, India has an extensive network of double tax conventions with industrialised as well as developing countries. There are 36 comprehensive conventions for avoidance of double taxation on income and 19 limited agreements in respect of taxes on income of airlines and shipping companies. Of the 36 comprehensive conventions, 15 had been entered prior to 1980. 21 new and 9 revised conventions have been entered after 1980. A double convention with USA awaits ratification by the US Senate. The conventions concluded by India substantially deviate from the UN or OECD models. The particular features of bilateral economic relations have influenced some of the convention terms. The convention with the United States follows, in many respects, the US model.

1. India has not entered into a separate exchange of information treaty with any country.

2. The main features of the post-1980 Indian tax conventions are discussed as follows:

N.B. The words 'treaty', 'convention', 'agreement' are used interchangeably and may not be read as indicating any difference.

2.1 Source rule and levy of tax on gross basis: The source rule has always been predominant in Indian double tax treaties. Prior to 1976 some treaties provided for taxation of technical service fees in the host country only insofar as the fees were attributable to services rendered in that country. In the absence of a specific provision relating to technical services in some treaties, the taxability depended on whether there was a permanent establishment in the host country - the criterion applicable to business profits. In 1976 the domestic tax law underwent significant changes. Technical service fees are now taxable at source irrespective of where the services are rendered, if the services are utilised in any business in India. Royalties, too, whether recurring or a lump sum, are in all circumstances taxable at source in India.

2.1.1 The tax is levied as specified percentage of the gross sum. The specified rate initially was 40% of the gross royalty or technical services fee.

The rate of tax agreed in the post-1976 treaties was generally 30%. In the case of the Federal Republic of Germany royalty was agreed to be taxed at the rate provided in the statute, while the rate for technical service fees was specified at 20%. Since 1987, the tax rate is reduced to 30% in the statute and, therefore, the treaties entered thereafter specify a rate of 20%. Those entered earlier continue to carry the 30% rate until the treaty countries seek revision. Revision of the rate to 20% should be almost automatic, subject to settlement of any treaty related pending issues.

2.1.2 To take care of such developments, it may be worthwile entering an understanding in the protocol along with the treaty that if, subsequent to entering the treaty, the domestic tax rate is reduced, the treaty rate will correspondingly stand reduced.

2.1.3 In the case of the US the rate of tax on royalties and 'included services' is reduced to 20%, with further agreement for reduction of the rate to 15% after a five year period. The expression 'included services' is narrower than 'technical services' and the scope is explained with examples in the protocol.

2.1.4 Interest and dividends are taxed on the source rule at 15% of the gross sum, *i.e.*, a rate which is 10 percentage points lower than the rate provided in the statute.

2.2 Permanent establishment: Industrial or commercial profits of a treaty country are taxable in the host country only insofar as they are attributable to a permanent establishment in the host country. The definition of permanent establishment in the post-1976 treaties is generally following the UN model. As a matter of policy, foreign companies except banking companies are not allowed to do business in India through a branch. The fee for supervisory services is any way taxed at source on gross basis. Widening of the concept of p.e. is, therefore, not of much relevance.

2.2.1 There is considerable litigation on the tax consequences of foreign companies having agency arrangements in India. Partly the reason is that the concept of p.e. does not figure in the domestic statute. Under the statute all income accruing or arising, whether directly or indirectly through or from any 'business connection', is taxable in India. The expression 'business connection' has a wide and uncertain meaning. Often, the assessing officers and tax counsel are not as familiar with tax treaty provisions and, therefore, mix up the concept of p.e. and 'business connection' leading to avoidable tax imposition and litigation.

2.3 Transfer pricing: Except for incorporating in the treaties the standard Article relating to 'Associated Enterprises', there are, for the present, no provisions or rules in the domestic statute or in the treaties specific to transfer pricing. The subject is however, currently under study by Government for suitable action.

2.4 Treaty consequences of measures to integrate taxes on corporations and shareholders: There is no attempt to integrate taxes on corporations and shareholders. The dividend income in the hands of non-corporate shareholders is taxed as ordinary income. Intercorporate dividends are exempted from tax to the extent the company distributing dividend has income from intercorporate dividends. In some treaties, like in the case of the UK, there is provision for tax credit in certain circumstances for underlying tax paid by the corporation in addition to credit for tax withheld as dividend tax in India.

2.5 Capital gains: The source rule applies to capital gains. Some problems have been arising in the case of capital gains arising on the alienation of shares in an Indian company by one non-resident to another. Problems relate to determination of the fair market value of shares, implications under the Gift Tax Act, consequences of currency devaluation losses, etc. The event leading to capital gains is expressed as 'alienation of property' in some treaties, and sale, exchange, or transfer in some others. Under the domestic law capital gains arise on 'transfer' of a capital asset and the inclusive definition of the world 'transfer' is very wide under the statute. This has been seen as causing some problems in tax assessments.

2.6 Exchange of information: A clause exists in all treaties almost in the same terms for exchange of information. In the pre-1980 treaties the exchange of information could only be for the purpose of carrying out the provisions of the agreement. In post-1980 treaties it is also for prevention of fraud or tax avoidance. The mutual cooperation regarding the operation of the Article is reported by the Revenue to be satisfactory.

2.7 Administrative assistance: Provision for extending any administrative assistance, say in the matter of collection of taxes or joint assessment, etc., rarely figures in any of the treaties. The treaty with Belgium is an exception where Article XXVII obligates the contracting States to extend to each other assistance in the collection of tax as if it were their own tax.

2.8 Methods to resolve conflicts: The treaties invariably provide for a mutual agreement procedure. At the request of a contracting State the competent authority may, by mutual agreement with the competent authority of the other contracting State, endeavour to resolve any difficulty or doubt arising as to the interpretation or application of the convention. The mutual agreement procedure has been satisfactorily invoked in some cases, but the instances are not many. Psychologically, perhaps, the competent authority procedure is considered complicated and not as accessible as the local appellate procedure handled by local consultants. There seems to be scope for invoking this procedure with advantage. Presently there are no provisions for international arbitration or joint audit.

ISSUES FOR DISCUSSION

3. Are double tax conventions in the best interest of developing countries? Are capital exporting countries interested?

Compliance with taxes of another country can never be taken lightly. Double tax conventions make such compliance easier and enable the taxpayer to determine his liability in advance with relative certainty. Unilateral double tax relief provisions generally existing in all tax jurisdictions are often not sufficient. The double tax conventions do make life easier for the taxpayers of the two countries. They are, therefore, of interest to both the industrialised and developing countries. The intensity of desire to negotiate and enter a treaty is, of course, determined by the extent of existing and potential economic interaction between the two countries for their mutual advantage.

It is doubtful whether any additional administrative burden is case on the Revenue by a tax treaty - of course, so long as one contracting State does not make undue demand on the other State for, say, exchange of information. Reciprocity is vital both at the stage of negotiating the treaty and for its operation.

3.1 Treaty negotiation procedure: Treaty negotiations, from experience, are prolonged indefinitely. Relatively small issues are carried over from one meeting to another. Tax being a technical subject, the negotiating teams comprising tax administrators sometimes tend not to take a broader view of the matters. It is for consideration whether the negotiating teams should include a professional economist. It may be useful to circulate a draft of the proposed treaty among relevant business and expert organisations for comments and suggestions.

3.2 Attitude to tax sparing: India has always insisted on tax-sparing provisions in double tax conventions. In principle insistance on tax sparing is rational, for otherwise the tax intended to be spared in favour of a foreign investor as inducement to invest in the host country does not benefit the investor but instead benefits the Revenue in the investor's country. Lately, however, with the trend towards substantial tax reduction in most industrialised countries, the tax-sparing provision is losing significance. India conceded ground on this issue in the treaty with the United States. Notwithstanding this case, the rationale of tax sparing must be duly appreciated.

3.3 Gross income taxes: In all post-1976 tax treaties it has concluded, India has insisted on a gross basis of withholding tax on royalties, technical service fees, dividends and interest. In recent years more and more provisions have been introduced in India for taxing non-residents on an assumed income basis. A foreign company engaged in civil construction or erection of plant and machinery in connection with an approved turnkey power project is effectively taxed at 6.5% of the gross total payment received in respect of the project. A similar provision applies for tax on exploration of mineral oils, shipping and operation of aircraft. Non-residents seem happy with this mode of levying tax because this makes the Indian tax liability certain, and accordingly allows for it to be included in the cost for work quotations. Even if the treaties do not incorporate the aforesaid, the taxpayer may opt for being taxed on the basis provided in the statute if he considers this more favourable than the usual basis of taxing of income of a permanent establishment.

3.4 Foreign exchange rate issues: Computation of taxable income, especially computation of capital gains in Indian Rupees, is often considered inequitable by foreign investors. While they sometimes receive less than their investment in their home country's currency, they are required to part with tax on account of capital gains in Rupee terms. There are no clear cut rules for computation of income in such cases. Whether the gain should first be computed in the currency of the investor and only the difference converted into Indian Rupees to serve as a basis for Indian capital gains tax, has been a debated issue. The treaties make no provision in this regard.

4. Proceeding on the premise that double tax conventions are in the mutual interest of industrialised as well as developing countries and that the Seminar will encourage entering into such conventions, the following points may merit discussion and suitable recommendation to secure the smooth and effective implementation of a convention.

4.1 Harmonious interpretation of convention provisions: For efficient and fair application of tax conventions, courts everywhere should attempt to interpret the provisions consistently, avoiding collision. The courts should, as far as possible, accept international precedents in interpreting the provisions of the conventions. Developments the world over in the interpretation of treaty provisions should receive due attention and adequate publicity.

4.2 Training and education: Tax administrators as well as tax practitioners, especially in developing countries, normally do not have day to day exposure to double tax conventions and, therefore, often lack adequate familiarity with them. Special training courses may be promoted for efficient and fair application of treaty provisions.

4.3 Use of protocol accompanying the treaty for recording the understanding reached between parties relating to various Articles in a treaty: A very elaborate protocol accompanies the recent Indo-US Tax Treaty, recording the understanding between parties regarding various Articles in the Treaty. The understanding reached is explained through examples. This provides useful guidance both to taxpayers and tax authorities in interpreting the Articles.

A protocol may take care of issues like the following:

4.3.1 Treaty vs statute: The Indian position is that double tax convention provisions override the provisions of the statute, if there is any conflict. This should hold good even in respect of any amendments to the statute subsequent to the Treaty, provided that the new statutory provisions are not more favorable than the treaty provisions. The understanding between the parties in this regard may be recorded in the protocol.

4.3.2 The mutual agreement procedure may be elaborated on in the protocol. A time-frame may be agreed within which the competent authorities will attempt to resolve any conflict.

4.3.3. The computation of income *vis-à-vis* foreign exchange rate issues can be outlined.

4.3.4 The tax credit system in each country may be usefully explained in the protocol. The extent of the tax credit is taken into account in negotiating business terms. The party entitled to tax credit often claims that full tax credit is not likely to be received by the party, especially where tax is withheld at source on gross basis. The other party reluctantly, but with reservation, accepts. This is not conducive to mutual trust and confidence. It would be useful, if the rules governing the tax credit could be made transparent to both the parties.

4.3.5 Expatriates deputed to provide supervisory services on any construction, erection, or assembly contract are subject to tax on their remuneration in the host country. The tax burden may, sometimes, be intolerable if the entire remuneration received by an expatriate in the home country, including social security and other contributions and benefits, is taken into account to compute his taxable salary in the host country. Neither the statute nor the treaty provisions provide appropriate relief in the computation of taxable income. If such expatriates are on secondment to the project, disputes arise on the issue whether the part of the remuneration paid in the home country, be it as a retention allowance or in any other form, is or is not taxable in the host country. The protocol may provide for an understanding between the parties on such and other issues.

BRIEF SURVEY OF THE DEVELOPMENT AND MAIN FEATURES OF THE UNITED KINGDOM'S DOUBLE TAXATION AGREEMENTS WITH DEVELOPING COUNTRIES

M.H. Collins (United Kingdom)

A. General Pattern of the UK's Agreements

1. The UK has made over fifty comprehensive agreements or arrangements for the prevention of double taxation with developing countries (including countries which until recently were described as Eastern Bloc countries).

2. The first such arrangements - a fairly sizeable number - were made in 1947, 1949 and the early 1950's, with what were then UK colonies or dependencies. Some which were made then still exist unamended. Some from that era have been amended in minor respects, so as, for example, to take account of changes in the tax laws of the partner countries, but are still basically the same in content. Others which were made at that time, on the other hand, have been comprehensively re-negotiated. In addition a number of completely new agreements have been negotiated with developing countries as the years have passed - mostly within the last twenty years. The UK's agreements with developing countries therefore vary quite widely in both form and content.

3. Looking generally at these agreements it is clear that there has been a considerable and continuing development over the years in the basic pattern. Nevertheless the basic pattern has always been conformable in most important matters with the thinking underlying the OECD Models - with variations designed to meet as far as possible the situation of each of the particular developing countries concerned.

4. The early agreements with the UK's dependencies took a comparatively simple form. They could perhaps be regarded as a less developed version of what later became the OECD Models, particularly in relation to the definition of a permanent establishment, the taxation of business profits, the treatment of profits of associated enterprises and the taxation of royalties. They differed from the Models, of course, in their drafting, but, for the most part, they contained the same essential features as the Models. One important difference was, however, that they contained no interest article (leaving the source country to tax the interest if its law so provided, and providing relief for that tax in the residence country; in the case of the UK by way of credit). Another difference was that the arrangements exempted dividends in both countries from source country taxation. A further difference was that they very rarely included a non-discrimination article.

5. Agreements made later, and comprehensive revisions of the earlier arrangements tended, however, to use the OECD Models as the effective negotiating basis, not only in following the more extended drafting pattern of the Models but also in allowing the source country to tax dividends (subject to a rate limitation), in limiting the source country's taxation of interest, and in including a non-discrimination article. In particular instances too they diverged from the OECD Model in order to meet various requirements of the developing country concerned - for example allowing the source country to tax royalties (though subject to a rate limitation) and in extending the definition of permanent establishment.

6. As time passed, these variations to meet the other country's requirements included features which were being considered for inclusion in the Guidelines then being worked out by the UN, or which had already been published among the UN Guidelines, and later still have included provisions figuring in the UN Model itself. For example, as already mentioned, the UK has frequently accepted the limited source taxation of royalties in agreements with developing countries. (But this acceptance is not confined to agreements with developing countries: it appears in some UK agreements with OECD countries as well.) The UK has also, several times, accepted (though perhaps reluctantly) the UN Model's inclusion of the furnishing of services within the definition of a permanent establishment, and has accepted too the UN's explicit exclusion of intra-entity royalties and interest from the deductible expenses of a permanent establishment.

B. Specific Provisions in the UK's Agreements

7. The basic pattern of the UK's agreements with developing countries remains nevertheless the OECD Model (plus a number of special features) rather than the UN Model. The UK's agreements with developing countries do however contain a number of special features which do not normally appear in the UK's agreements with other countries and which do not appear in the OECD Models or in the UN Model. These include such comparatively minor points, for example, as the explicit acceptance in some agreements that a sales outlet is a permanent establishment, and that a warehouse is a permanent establishment in relation to a person providing storage for other persons. They also include the acceptance in some agreements that a building or construction site is a permanent establishment not only where it exists for twelve months (the OECD Model) or where it exists for six months (the UN Model), but also where it exists for a shorter period in certain circumstances.

8. However, probably the two most important special features appearing in such agreements are

(a) the treatment of technical etc. fees as a separate class of gross income, and

(b) the provision by the UK of tax relief to UK taxpayers to match reliefs given to those taxpayers by the partner developing country in order to encourage development - the so-called tax-sparing relief or matching credit.

9. Technical etc fees

Some developing countries prefer to tax fees paid to non-residents for management, technical or consultancy services as gross income, and thus to treat them effectively in the same way as royalties by subjecting them to withholding tax at a flat rate. In a number of its agreements with such countries the UK has gone along with this. Usually however the UK seeks to ensure that the recipient has the option of being taxed only on his net income from the fees, that is to say, as if he had a permanent establishment in the source country. Where such provisions are included, the method of arriving at the net income on this basis is left to be worked out by the relevant tax authority as best it can in the light of the circumstances and the arguments of the taxpayer. But in some cases where the agreement contains a technical fees article the UK has accepted a flat rate withholding tax with no net income option.

10. Tax-sparing relief

Since 1961, the UK has been prepared to include tax-sparing provisions in an agreement with a developing country if this is consistent with producing a balanced treaty overall, and more than thirty of the UK's agreements include such provisions. The legislation authorising their inclusion enables the relief to be given only in relation to reliefs provided in the other country under legislation designed to promote industrial, commercial, scientific, educational or other development. Thus the UK has agreed to provide matching relief for tax spared in respect of clearly defined development projects which will patently help the partner country strengthen its economic and industrial base. The UK has not provided matching relief for relief given under legislation specifically designed to promote exports, and it has never conceded 'across-the-board' matching credit for tax (such as withholding tax on dividends or interest) given up by the partner country under the terms of the agreement.

11. Other provisions

(a) It may be helpful here to consider briefly the treatment of a number of other important issues in the UK's agreements with developing countries.

(b) Source rules: Source rules do not figure largely in the UK's agreements. The OECD Model rule for defining the source of interest is often used however, and, analogously, so too are similar rules for defining the source of royalties and,

where appropriate, the source of technical, management and consultancy fees.

(c) *The arm's length principle and transfer pricing:* The UK's agreements (whether they are with developing or developed countries) deal with the taxation of branch profits and the profits of associated enterprises by reference to the arm's length principle, as do both the OECD and the UN Models. Where associated enterprises are involved there is provision for adjustments to be made to transfer prices to arrive at arm's length profits, but no detailed rules are supplied, and the fullest scope is left to the tax authorities to find satisfactory ways in which to implement the provision - no doubt bearing in mind the guidance given by the OECD in its 1979 Transfer Pricing Report and subsequent studies and the similar guidance produced in the Report of the UN Expert Groups. In some cases the UK agreements provide scope for corresponding adjustments to be made by the other country, usually under an equivalent to Article (9)(2) of the OECD and UN Models - but not mandatorily. In other agreements an equivalent relief is provided in the UK under the article in the agreement corresponding to Article 23 of the OECD and UN Models - Elimination of Double Taxation.

(d) Integration of company profits and distributions: The partial integration of taxes on corporate profits and on shareholders' dividends is a feature of UK tax law. Under the UK's tax agreements there is basically no taxation of dividends in the hands of the shareholder when the shareholder is non-resident. But when, as is commonly the case where the shareholder controls less than ten per cent of the voting power in the company paying the dividend, and is sometimes the case in other circumstances, the shareholder can claim, under the agreement, in addition to his dividend, a credit in respect of the UK tax suffered by the company on its profits, then tax may be charged, usually at a maximum rate of fifteen per cent, though less if less than the full credit can be claimed, on the aggregate of the dividend plus credit. Any limitation of the rate of tax chargeable by the partner country on dividends payable from sources therein to residents of the UK is clearly negotiated with this factor among others in mind.

(e) Capital gains: The UK's agreements tend to approach the treatment of capital gains by restricting the right of each partner country to tax residents of the other country to the right to tax gains arising from the alienation of immovable property (or of property attributable to a permanent establishment or fixed base) situated in that partner country – thus excluding the right provided in the UN Model to tax gains arising to a non-resident from the alienation of shares in a resident company. UK agreements do sometimes however permit the taxation by one country of gains arising to a resident of the other, in addition to immovable property gains or gains arising from the alienation of property attributable to a permanent establishment or fixed base, if that person was at some time in the recent past (say, five, or possibly ten years before) a resident of the country seeking to tax him.

(f) Exchange of information: The UK's comprehensive double taxation agreements whether with developed or developing countries, all contain an article pro-

viding exchange of information between the competent authorities of the two countries. The drafting varies to some extent but the provision is essentially the same in all the agreements and resembles very closely the OECD Model's Article 26.

(g) Administrative assistance: None of the UK's agreements specify what sort of administrative assistance the competent authorities may provide for each other in operating the agreement apart from exchange of information. This is left to be worked out by the competent authorities in direct consultation with each other. The UK does not provide assistance to other countries in the collection of their tax (the assistance provided under the treaty with the USA is by way of collecting UK tax which would otherwise be given up by relief at source).

(h) Mutual consultation: Where a taxpayer feels that he has not been treated satisfactorily under one of the UK's agreements (whether this is with a developing or a developed country) the mutual consultation provisions in the agreement go no further than to permit the competent authorities to consult together with a view to seeking a solution to whatever problem may be involved. The UK competent authority cannot accept or implement a solution which does not fall within the UK law. Specific mutual agreement articles did not always appear in the earlier agreement made by the UK. It does not appear however that the absence of such an article prevents the UK from entering into consultation with the other country's competent authorities.

(i) Students and teachers: The UK in all its comprehensive agreements provides some relief from tax for payments made for the maintenance of visiting students or apprentices (a feature of both the OECD and the UN Models), and, in a majority of the agreements, provides also some relief from tax for the emoluments of visiting professors or teachters, or, in some cases, research workers (provisions which are not a feature of either the OECD or the UN Model). It has been the UK's practice to include such provisions ever since it began to negotiate comprehensive agreements so Part of the reason for this is no doubt the help which it is thought that such provisions may give to developing countries by encouraging their students and apprentices to study in the UK. Similarly it has no doubt been argued that the reciprocal exemptions for teachers are helpful to developing countries in encouraging UK teachers to work in their countries. (In addition of course it can be argued that the UK gets reciprocal benefits from exchanges of experience and skills in the opposite directions.)

General Issues for Discussion

A. Value of Double Taxation Agreements

12. There has been for many years a wide recognition that international agreements designed to prevent double taxation are useful expedients for the facilitation of international trade and investment. The United Nations' Economic and Social Council expressed the need, in 1967, for measures to encourage the making of such agreements between developed and developing countries, and the UN Model which was drafted finally in 1979 was designed to facilitate the making of such treaties by providing a Model which was more suitable for the purpose than the OECD Model. It is perhaps appropriate to consider now, again, what value such agreements have for both taxpayers and tax authorities.

13. For the taxpayers of developed countries wishing to carry on trade or investment in developing countries the advantages are perhaps (apart from any limitation of the tax burden provided by the agreements) the advantages of clarity and certainty, advantages which are those of any agreement, whether between a developed and a developing country or between two developed countries. Where there is an agreement, taxpayers can, within certain limits, see, better than where there is no such agreement, what their tax position will be within the other country, and, in conjunction with their own country's domestic law, the extent to which they can be assured of relief from domestic tax in respect of such foreign tax as remains payable after the operation of the agreement. It would be wrong to exaggerate the importance of these advantages. They may not in fact be conclusive for traders or investors in arriving at a decision to trade or invest in another country. Sometimes in fact the process may work the other way: it may be the very existence of trade or investment by non-residents which stimulates a demand for an agreement. But, it may be argued, the making of such an agreement may well make those already trading or investing in a country readier to do so, and may influence them to increase their trade or investment as well as encouraging others to follow their example. Nevertheless, it is obvious that, if the circumstances are right, there can be massive investment of one sort or another by residents of developed countries in less developed countries without the assistance of double taxation agreements. It is no easy matter to measure the importance of such agreements to taxpayers in any particular case.

14. For the tax authorities of developed countries the advantages of double taxation agreements, whatever the state of development of the partner country, are primarily that limits are placed on the foreign tax for which they may be required to give relief. Secondarily, it may be an advantage, if this is what their Governments desire that, to a certain extent, the agreements make it easier for their taxpayers to trade and invest abroad. A third advantage may lie in an assurance that their taxpayers are being treated equitably in the taxation of their trading and investment activities abroad, and that they are not being required to give relief for tax which is not obviously equitably imposed. A fourth advantage, potentially at least, is that they may receive some assistance from the other country's authorities in the detection and prevention of fiscal fraud and evasion.

15. The fact that many developed countries each have an extensive tax treaty network seems to indicate that these and possibly other advantages are found to be worth having.

16. Treaty shopping

But the existence of such extended networks of agreements with often substantially different terms applying to the same kinds of income has exposed some developed countries to the danger that taxpayers will seek to channel their international transactions through treaty partner countries in such a way that they benefit in every case from the most advantageous treaty. Some such countries have consequently sought to include provisions in their treaties which will minimise the advantages of such 'treaty shopping'. For developing countries however the problem has not yet seemed to be of general importance.

17. For the tax authorities and Governments of developing countries the extent of any advantage which they may derive from double taxation agreements with developed countries will thus depend, partly at any rate, on the extent of their perceived need to encourage development by way of trade and investment from abroad and their perception of the effectiveness of such agreements in providing such encouragement. A range of double taxation agreements with developed countries may be of value to a developing country, simply by providing an indication to potential traders and investors that the developing country is prepared to welcome such trade or investment. The advantages will be increased to the extent that the relevant developed countries are prepared to give relief for the developing country's tax, to take positive steps to prevent the frustration of the effects of the developing country's own tax reliefs, and to co-operate in enabling the developing country's tax authorities to impose tax effectively on foreign traders and investors.

B. The Usefulness of the United Nations' Model

18. In fact many double taxation agreements have been made between developed and developing countries and more continue to be made. On the assumption which this fact seems to bear out, that double taxation agreements between developed and developing countries have been found to be of value to developing countries, the question arises as to what effect the UN Model has had and can have in facilitating the process of negotiating such agreements. Does it in fact achieve the purpose envisaged for it by the UN ECOSOC in 1967 of facilitating 'the conclusion of tax treaties between developed and developing countries ... which would be acceptable to both groups of countries and would fully safeguard their respective revenue interests.'?

19. The Model is a compromise between the views of experts from both groups of countries. It was only finalised after many years of difficult argument, and, while it clearly does not give the developing countries all that many of them would like to have, it represents, in the developed countries' view, a substantial modification of what ought to be contained in a balanced tax treaty (as exemplified by the OECD Model), particularly in the concessions which it makes to the source principle of taxation.

20. When the UN Expert Group in 1985 carried out a general view of the effectiveness of the UN Model, there was, nevertheless, a fair amount of agreement in the Group that the Model was useful in forming the basis for negotiations and had helped in the process of making agreements between developed and developing countries. On the other hand it is clear that the Model does not provide a complete template for every pair of developed and developing countries. Indeed some developed countries are prepared to go further than the Model does in some respects towards accommodating the point of view of the developing countries. Providing matching relief for tax spared and treating technical fees as gross income in certain circumstances are but two examples of this. On the other hand the same developed countries may well not be prepared to go along with the Model at all in other situations. It needs to be said however that developed countries negotiating with each other will often diverge from the OECD Model to suit the particular purposes of each partner country, and this is not regarded as a serious indication that the OECD Model is inadequate for its purpose.

21. It is perhaps the case, nevertheless, that the UN Model in its sphere is less influential than the OECD Model is in its sphere, and the question is sometimes raised whether the UN Model could be revised to make it more useful.

22. It seems unlikely that the Expert Group will in fact be able to agree on any substantial modifications of the Model, at any rate in the near future. Although the Model has no positive authority - it is expressly not an authorised or recommended Model of the United Nations - it does nevertheless have a kind of moral authority, in that the proposal in bilateral negotiations of a provision which does not appear in the Model, or the rejection of one which does, probably requires more justification than the proposal of one which does appear or the rejection of one which does not. Possibly, therefore, for this sort of reason, what may be acceptable as a compromise in the special circumstances of particular bilateral negotiations would often seem to be too sizeable a concession if expressed in a general form as a Model Article. Nevertheless the Group does keep the use of the Model under continuous review, and, by reporting from time to time on the various ways in which it has been found possible to extend or modify its terms in the course of negotiating bilateral treaties, the Group may, it is hoped, be able to point the way to acceptable compromises outside the Model, where it is apparent that these are really necessary.

23. Tax-sparing

The absence of a tax-sparing provision is possibly one of the more important omissions from the Model from the point of view of developing countries, though it is only of importance where the developed country partner gives relief to its own taxpayers by way of credit and not by way of exemption. But it is not the absence of a Model article which creates the difficulty of negotiating an agreement - the drafting of such an article is not difficult in itself - but the inability of the developed country concerned to make the necessary concession. How far this inability does in fact hold up the making of bilateral agreements is not easy to estimate, nor is it easy to say whether the denial of such a concession is as important now as it may have seemed in the past. That it has prevented or at least delayed the making of some agreements is undeniable.

24. Arguments against giving matching relief for spared tax include

(a) that the purpose of double taxation agreements is to relieve double taxation - in some cases by sharing the tax effectively between the partner countries - and not to provide taxpayers with a double relief, and

(b) that to undertake to give relief for foreign tax which is not in fact paid is to invite abuse by way of artificial 'soak-up' taxes - the partner developing country may be encouraged to raise the nominal level of the tax which it gives up to the real level of the other country's tax, so as to maximise the benefit to the taxpayer of the matching credit and thus maximise the investment incentive. However, some countries obviously regard double relief as either unimportant or as an acceptable expedient in certain circumstances, particularly where it is a question of help in developing the industry etc. of developing countries.

It is not easy to see how far there has in fact been a 'soak-up' reaction to the provision of matching relief for tax spared. But if there has been such a reaction it seems generally not to have deterred many developed countries from providing matching relief in the agreements with developing countries. In all this it is clear that different countries have different sticking points, and different conceptions of the extent to which they feel justified in giving assistance to developing countries through the mechanism of tax agreements.

C. Practical International Fiscal Co-operation

25. It goes without saying that the drafting and negotiation of tax agreements is only the first step in international fiscal cooperation. For the taxpayers concerned it is probably enough that satisfactory rules and reliefs are provided by the agreements - so long as they derive adequate advantages from them. For the Governments concerned however it may be of some importance that they should be able to use the agreements to protect their revenue - by, for example, minimising fiscal fraud and evasion. For developing countries it may be particularly important that they should be able to rely on the tax authorities of the partner country, where this is a developed country, to help them, by using the Exchange of Information article in the relevant treaty, to deal satisfactorily with international tax evasion and avoidance and with the transfer prices involved in transactions between relevant elements of multinational enterprises.

26. There can be advantages for the developed country partner in such exchanges too, but developing countries will perhaps feel more strongly that there is scope for growth in this area of international fiscal co-operation. Indeed this aspect of it may become one of the most important arguments in favour of making double taxation agreements between developed and developing countries in the future. This seems particularly the case bearing in mind the considerable distrust of the transfer pricing of multinationals which is felt by the tax authorities of both developing and developed countries. If multinational enterprises are not taxed properly on an arm's length basis the alternatives are to tax them unsystematically or arbitrarily and it does not seem plausible that either of these alternatives is likely to satisfy indefinitely the tax authorities (whether of developed or developing countries) or the taxpayers. The development of this kind of cooperation is however dependent on the countries concerned having an adequate skilled and experienced staff available to engage in the considerable amount of work necessary to make such cooperation effective. It takes time and resources to build up such a staff however and it may be necessary for tax authorities to recognize that progress in these matters may be slow.

27. When tax authorities get together the taxpayer may feel threatened. From the taxpayer's point of view it seems desirable therefore that exchanges of confidential information between tax authorities should be made, if at all, either under the terms or in association with a satisfactory agreement for the relief of double taxation, so as to ensure as far as possible that such exchanges result only in fair taxation and do not result in unrelievable double taxation.

28. For taxpayers too there may thus appear to be a growing need, not only for an effective use to be made of the mutual consultation provisions in bilateral treaties to enable them to defend themselves against the unsatisfactory implementation of the treaties, differences of interpretation between the competent authority misunderstandings on transfer pricing and so forth, but also for a mechanism which can resolve differences between the competent authorities which may lead to unfair taxation or unrelieved double taxation and which the normal processes of consultation cannot resolve. This need does not appear to be an especially pressing one at present, but if it does become more important it is not likely to be confined to agreements between developed and developing countries. It is interesting that the member countries of the European Communities (the EC) have in fact recently signed a treaty providing a mechanism for resolving such differences between themselves. What may deter many countries from accepting such a mechanism however is the loss of sovereignty involved.

UNITED STATES VIEWS ON SELECTED ASPECTS OF DEVELOPING COUNTRY TAX TREATY ISSUES*

M.S. Feinberg (USA)

I. United States Views on tax-sparing Credits

The United States does not include tax sparing credits, or other explicit forms of investment incentive in any tax treaties. United States objection to tax sparing is based on both tax policy concerns and concerns relating to more general economic or legislative policy.

US policy of not granting US benefits to US persons

It is US policy that, with limited exceptions, US tax treaties provide US benefits only to residents of the partner and not to US residents. It is the partner's concessions which benefit US persons. Tax sparing credits would clearly violate this policy. This policy grows largely out of the US Constitutional requirements that tax legislation must originate in the House of Representatives, the lower house, but only the Senate, the upper house, has a formal role in the process of treaty approval. Furthermore, within the Senate, it is the Foreign Relations Committee, and not the tax-writing Finance Committee, that plays the key role. This division of tax policy responsibilities among arms of the US legislature led to the decision many years ago that treaties could, by action only of the Senate, affect US taxation of foreign persons, but US taxation of US persons would, as a general matter, remain a legislative responsibility in which both houses participate.

The Senate has, on several occassions, objected to relatively insignificant grants of US treaty benefits to US Persons. It is clear that it would strongly oppose granting a benefit as important as tax sparing to US residents by treaty.

Capital export neutrality

A major economic objective of US tax treaty policy is that of fostering capital export neutrality, *i.e.*, allowing investment location decisions to be based on market, not tax, considerations. Tax sparing conflicts with this policy objective.

* *The views expressed are those of the author, and do not necessarily reflect those of the US Treasury Department.*

Encouraging investment in developing countries by reducing tax impediments to capital flows, thus allowing market forces to be more determinative in the investment location decision, is consistent with this policy. It is not, however, consistent to encourage investment decisions which would not be made but for the tax incentive. Government policies should not encourage inefficient resource allocation even if such allocation is consistent with a policy of encouraging economic development. Other, more economically sound measures or programs must be sought to achieve this objective.

Importance of tax-sparing to potential investors

The importance of US tax-sparing to developing countries seems to rest, at least in part, on a misperception of the operation of the US tax system, and particularly the foreign tax credit. Developing countries see any reduction in their tax as causing a dollar-for-dollar reduction in the US foreign tax credit, and, thus, a dollar-for-dollar increase in the investor's US tax after credit. They see their tax concessions, therefore, as doing no more than transfering revenues from their Treasury to the US Treasury, leaving no benefit for the US investor.

When analyzed in the context of the US taxation of foreign source income, it is not clear that, in a broad range of cases, tax sparing would afford a significant benefit to US investors. There are features of US law that tend to mitigate the dollar-for-dollar offset effect of the foreign tax credit. The position taken by certain American business groups that a treaty without tax-sparing is far preferable to no treaty lends support to the view that features of US law render tax-sparing credits less important to US firms than they may at first appear to be.

The effects of deferral

The most important of these aspects of US law is deferral. A US investor is not generally subject to US tax on the earnings of a foreign subsidiary until those earnings are repatriated to the United States. Current US taxation of controlled foreign corporation profits under subpart F of the Internal Revenue Code generally does not apply to the kinds of investments which are eligible for developing country tax holidays. Thus, in the typical case, as long as tax holiday profits are not repatriated, there is no US tax and no offset to the tax holiday benefit. Deferral acts as an incentive to reinvest low-taxed profits. This is clearly in the development interest of the host developing country.

When the deferred tax holiday profits are ultimately repatriated, US tax will apply, subject to both a direct foreign tax credit for any withholding tax, and a deemed paid credit for underlying corporate tax. The deemed paid credit is based on the average foreign tax paid with respect to the pool of accumulated profits out of which the dividend is paid. Assume, for example, a 5-year tax holiday during which a total of $1000 of tax-free profits are earned and reinvested. In year 6, profits of $250 are earned and are subject to a 50 percent income tax. The $125 of after-tax profits are distributed in that year, subject to a 15 percent withholding tax ($18.75). The average underlying income tax rate for the 6 year period for purposes of the deemed-paid credit is 10 percent ($125 of tax and $1,250 of profits). The dividend of $125, therefore, would carry a deemed paid credit of $12.50 and a direct credit of $18.75. US taxable income would be $137.50 (the dividend grossed-up by the deemed-paid tax). The US corporate income tax at a 34 percent rate would be $ 46.75, and after a foreign tax credit of $31.25 the net tax would be $15.50. Thus, if the investor reinvests profits during the tax holiday period and repatriates current profits after the holiday ends, there would, in the example, be some US tax consequence, but significantly less than a dollar-for-dollar offset. Moreover, tax holiday benefits are enjoyed to the extent that profits are reinvested. Even if there is some US tax on subsequent repatriation of the deferred profits, the investor has received the significant economic benefit of deferring payment of US tax.

Effects of the foreign tax credit limitation

If the investor chooses not to reinvest, but to repatriate the tax holiday profits currently, the overall foreign tax credit limitation may, depending on circumstances, serve to shelter some or all of the tax holiday profits from US tax. If the developing country subsidiary is owned more than 50 percent by a US investor, the dividend income from that corporation will go into the general foreign tax credit basket, meaning that the income and foreign tax from that investment will be grouped with the income and foreign tax from other overseas investments of the US investor. To the extent that there is high-taxed income in the basket from the same or another country, such as dividends from a high-tax-country subsidiary, the tax-holiday dividends will be averaged with the high-taxed dividends in determining the limit for the investor's foreign tax credit. The tax-holiday income may thus be fully or partially sheltered from US tax by the excess foreign tax credits generated with respect to the high-taxed income.

The 1986 foreign tax credit limitation changes have made the sheltering described in the previous paragraph more difficult. The variety of separate baskets provided for foreign tax credit limitation purposes, particularly, in this context, the separate limitation on dividends from non-controlled foreign subsidiaries, have increased the circumstances where possibilities for averaging high and low taxed foreign income may not be present. The potential for benefit, nonetheless, remains in a broad range of cases.

Tax-sparing encourages inefficient tax and development policies

It is not clear that tax sparing is in the development interest of developing countries. First, as noted, to benefit from tax sparing the investor must repatriate profits, while deferral of US tax without tax sparing encourages reinvestment of profits. Reinvestment, not repatration, is what developing countries should be seeking. Furthermore, tax sparing encourages countries with serious revenue shortfalls to exacerbate their problems by granting tax holidays. There is no clear economic evidence that tax holidays are of major significance in attracting capital. The availability of resources and a skilled labor force, access to markets and a minimum of administrative regulation and confusion probably far outweigh taxes in importance in investment location decisions.

Investors in a country with relatively low tax rates applied generally, a system which many would consider rational, cannot benefit from tax sparing. Investment, however, in a country with a less efficient system of high tax rates but many tax holiday exceptions would stand to benefit from tax sparing.

Finally, tax sparing generates benefits to an investor only if and when an investment becomes profitable and generates a return flow of income.

Level of benefits not under control of country granting benefits

Under a tax sparing regime, the level of benefits granted by the capital exporting country to its investors depends not on its policies, but on the tax policies of the developing, capital importing, country. The broader the range of activities eligible for tax holidays in the developing country, the longer the holiday period and the higher the nominal tax rate in the developing country relative to the effective rate under the tax holiday, the greater is the benefit. These features are all determined by the developing country. If the United States is to provide tax benefits for investment in developing countries, it is argued, the scope of those benefits should be within the control of the United States Government.

II. Permanent Establishment/Business Profits Issues

Although foreign branch operations tend to be relatively few in number, outside the financial sector, permanent establishment/business profits provisions of developing country treaties are among the most hard-fought issues in negotiations. Many developing countries have low internal law threshold tests for taxing the business profits of a foreign enterprise. In some cases little more than direct sales into the country from abroad or the performances of services abroad on behalf of a client in the developing country can give rise to an income tax liability of the foreign enterprise.

The United States has two fundamental objectives in the permanent establishment/business profits provisions of treaties with developing countries. The first is to set the permanent establishment thresholds sufficiently high, recognizing the partner's interest in establishing very low thresholds, to permit an enterprise to explore a market in the partner country by engaging in limited activities there without becoming involved in the country's tax system. This avoids not only the payment of host country tax, but, perhaps more important, the need to become involved in what are frequently complex, or at least new, administrative procedures. If these exploratory activities prove successful, they can be expected to expand to a point where they will rise to the level of a permanent establishment and the income generated from the activities will become subject to host country tax. Absent the initial insulation from host country tax, the exploratory activities are less likely to take place.

The second objective is to assure that where an enterprise's business income is taxable by the partner under the treaty, tax will be imposed on an appropriate basis. That is, only income attributable to the permanent establishment will be subject to tax, and tax will be imposed on a net basis, with host country deductions allowed for all reasonably connected expenses, wherever incurred. This can be accomplished by clarifying that certain classes of income (*e.g.*, income from the rental of movable property or income from services) are treated as business profits. It is also important to clarify the obligation to allow reasonable expenses in computing business profits.

It is sometimes necessary to include in the permanent establishment definition special rules to determine when activities which give rise to certain classes of income will constitute a permanent establishment. For example, the permanent establishment definition may include a special time threshold for income from the provision of personal services which will cause a permanent establishment to be present, even if, under standard rules, absent this special provision, no permanent establishment would exist. The inclusion of such provision has two consequences. It allows host country tax when the threshold test is met, but in doing so it assures that the income in question will be treated as business profits and, therefore, will be taxable on a net basis. Absent such provisions, many countries will subject the income to gross basis tax at source, frequently with no threshold.

Delivery of goods or merchandise

A significant problem for the United States arises from a provision of Article 5(4) of the UN Model which deviates from the OECD and US Models. Sub-paragraphs (a) and (b) provide that the use of facilities or the maintenance of a stock of goods for the purpose of storage or display does not constitute a permanent establishment. The OECD and US Models speak of storage, display *or delivery*. Under the UN Model, therefore, the use of facilities or the maintenance of a stock of goods or merchandise merely for the purpose of delivering the goods or merchandise could constitute a permanent establishment. The United States considers this an inappropriate result. Consider the following example: a US company sells a product directly to residents of a developing country, with no sales activity or presence in that country. There is no permanent establishment and no local tax on the US company's income. If, instead of shipping each item directly to the purchasers, the US company seeks to facilitate the process by shipping several of the items to an independent warehouse in the developing country for subsequent delivery from the warehouse to each purchaser, the absence of the word 'delivery' would result in the US company having a permanent establishment and being subject to tax. It is difficult to distinguish these cases substantively. Furthermore, it is difficult to identify the income properly attributable to the permanent establishment in the latter case.

Some developing countries insist on some change from the OECD Model with respect to 'delivery'. In such cases, the preferred US position has been to provide that delivery does not constitute a permanent establishment except where the delivery is effected through a store or other sales outlet. Where the partner insists on a still more restrictive provision, the United States has agreed to delete the word 'delivery', but has insisted on adding language which says, 'Notwithstanding the preceding provisions of the article, the term ''permanent establishment'' shall be deemed not to include the use of facilities or the maintenance of a stock of goods or merchandise belonging to the enterprise for the purpose of occasional delivery of such goods or merchandise.' This requires a sometimes difficult distinction to be made between regular and occasional delivery.

Dependent agents

A similar problem arises with the UN Model provision for determining when the use by an enterprise of a dependent agent constitutes a permanent establishment of that enterprise. In the OECD and US Models, an enterprise will have a permanent establishment through the activities of a dependent agent only when the agent has and exercises an authority to conclude contracts in the name of the enterprise. The UN Model broadens this to add that even if the agent has no such authority, he will constitute a permanent establishment if he maintains a stock of goods or merchanidse from which the regularly makes deliveries on behalf of the enterprise. As with the UN Model provision relating to 'delivery', the United States has taken the view that this provision gives the host country too broad a taxing right. As an alternative, the United States has agreed to this provision, but with the addition of the following words: '... and additional activities conducted in that State on behalf of the enterprise have contributed to the sale of the goods or merchandise.' This requires some sales activity to have taken place in the host country, in addition to delivery, though it need not be the agent who has carried on those activities.

Independent agents

The independent agent provisions of the UN Model also pose problems for the United States by broadening the circumstances under which such an agent will constitute a permanent establishment. The OECD and US Models look only at the economic relationship between the agent and the enterprise in determining whether the agency relationship is dependent or independent. The UN Model adds that an otherwise independent agent will be considered dependent, and thus a permanent establishment of the enterprise, if the activities of the agent are devoted wholly or almost wholly on behalf of the enterprise. This can result in the unjustified characterization of an independent agent as dependent. For example, if an independent agent represents several enterprises, including enterprise A, the agent would not be a permanent establishment of A. If all of the agent's clients except A decide to take their business elsewhere, A would suddenly find itself with a permanent establishment even though nothing had changed in its business dealings in the host country or in its relationship with the agent. As a compromise, the United States has accepted the UN version in several treaties with the addition of a rule which requires that transactions between the agent and the enterprise were not made under arm's-length conditions. The presence of non-arm's-length conditions implies some dependent relationship between the agent and the enterprise.

Definition of business profits

Some of the most difficult problems in developing country negotiations are those relating to the definition of business profits. Many developing countries prefer to define business profits narrowly, in order to limit the classes of income subject to a permanent establishment threshold and taxable on a net basis. The classes of income which developing countries tend often to exclude from business profits are management fees and income from the rental of movable property. The United States considers both of these to be business profits. In developing countries, such classes of income are generally treated either as royalties or as a separate class of income taxable on a gross basis at source.

The UN Model does provide a permanent establishment rule for management fees, but this is one of the compromises in the UN Model which developing countries frequently find inadequate in preserving source country taxation. The UN Model provides that an enterprise which is furnishing services, through employees or other personnel, will have a permanent establishment in a country if the activities continue there for periods aggregating more than six months in a twelve-month period. The implication of this rule is that such income is business profits, taxable only on a net basis and only when attributable to a permanent establishment. The rule may have the effect of causing a permanent establishment to exist in circumstances where there would be none under the OECD Model. It is the latter feature which gives the rule some appeal to developing countries. To make the rule more acceptable the United States has, in some treaties agreed to reduce the time threshold to 90 days for services in general, and to zero where the services are performed for a related party.

The United States has dealt with income from the rental of movable property in some developing country treaties by incorporating a rule similar to the services rule described above. Under such a rule, the maintenance of substantial equipment by an enterprise of one Contracting State in the other for more than 120 consecutive days (whether for its own use or for use by others) will constitute a permanent establishment of the enterprise which owns the equipment. Thus, if a US computer manufacturer leases a computer to a developing country company for six months, the computer company would have a permanent establishment there, even if the presence of the computer there is its only connection with the host country, and the net lease income would be taxable. Absent this rule, under the OECD Model, the mere presence of the computer for six months would not give rise to a permanent establishment and the income could not be taxed. To further clarify that such income is to be treated as business profits, US treaties tend to define business profits to include income from the rental of tangible personal property. As with the services rule, the 120 days rental rule will cause a permanent establishment to exist in many circumstances where one would not exist absent that rule.

The absence of such rules poses several types of problems for developed country enterprises doing business in developing countries. Income which is properly business profits will not be treated as such. Expenses, which will frequently be high with respect to these types of income, will not be allowed. High rates of tax on gross income, therefore, will frequently translate into confiscatory rates on net income. Particularly with respect to service income, foreign tax will often be imposed on income which the United States treats as US source (*i.e.*, for services performed in the United States), thereby making the foreign tax non-creditable.

II. SUMMARY OF PROCEEDINGS

SUMMARY OF PROCEEDINGS OF THE SEMINAR 'DOUBLE TAXATION TREATIES BETWEEN INDUSTRIALISED AND DEVELOPING COUNTRIES: OECD AND UN MODELS, A COMPARISON'

written by Dr. Barry Bracewell-Milnes (UK) on the occasion of the 44th Congress, Stockholm, 1990 (29 August)

Professor Leif Mutén, United States, Chairman of the Seminar, said that the Panel consisted of tax administrators past or present. He introduced the Members of the Panel who were: - *Mr. M. Collins,* United Kingdom; *Mr. J.F. Court,* France; *Mr. Mordecai S. Feinberg,* United States; *Mr. A. Figueroa,* Argentina; *Mr. O.P. Vaish,* India. *Professor Mutén* said that the Seminar had been arranged to take stock of developments following the 1980 publication of the UN Model Tax Convention. The UN Model had come into existence in recognition of the fact that the OECD Model, which assumed reciprocity in the relations between treaty countries, was not altogether appropriate for treaty relationships where no reciprocity existed. In addition, for many developing countries an important part of the tax base consisted of international trade and inward investment activities: foreign ownership was important in the modern sector of the economy, expatriates were employed to a significant extent, services and knowhow were procured from foreign suppliers, and substantial interest and royalty payments were made to recipients abroad.

In these circumstances tax concessions involved forgoing significant amounts of tax revenue. So many questions that could be resolved in the OECD context on the basis of simplicity and practicability were seen in a different light in treaty relationships between industrialised and developing countries. Furthermore, the UN Model was the product of a group of experts not officially representing their governments nor representing all the developing or industrialised countries whose interests were at stake in the discussion. The importance of the issues and the limited mandate of the experts producing the Model had resulted in a Model Convention of a kind different from the OECD Model, leaving more to negotiation in each particular case. Moreover the UN Model, although it represented an impressive effort to come to terms with the many problems involved, was still not regarded by everyone as the final solution to all these problems. In evaluating the UN Model there was still a certain difference of opinion between the industrialised countries (represented on the Panel by three Members) and the developing countries (represented by two Members). The more positive evaluation of the UN Model on the part of the industrialised countries could perhaps be interpreted as a tacit admission that the UN Model was still too close to the OECD Model to be regarded as a real compromise by the developing countries.

Another and probably more realistic way of regarding the question was that the much smaller revenue significance of the issues for industrialised countries made for a more detached attitude on the part of these countries' representatives. The first part of the afternoon's discussion would be concerned with whether or not there was a need for treaties, and also with the question of tax sparing. After the coffee break there would be a discussion of permanent establishments and then the debate would be thrown open to participants from the floor. Papers by each of the five Panelists had been distributed before the start of the Seminar. *Mr. Figueroa*'s paper set out the reasoning of those who felt that the developing country representatives had been too forthcoming in the search for a compromise within the groups of experts, and who saw a general source country rule as the only practicable solution to the problem of double taxation. He invited Mr. Figueroa to speak on the question of whether or not there was a need for treaties.

Mr. Figueroa said that in the continuing discussions of the UN expert group he had by 1981 already noticed major differences between the experts from developing countries and those from industrialised countries. Those from industrialised countries had a homogeneous outlook; those from developing countries dit not. Some of the latter were most concerned about transfer prices, others about tariffs, and others again about the concept of permanent establishment, and so on; this led to the intellectual predominance of the industrialised countries' representatives in the discussions of the expert group. Turning to the question of whether it was necessary to have double tax treaties in order to attract inward investment, he said that it was not. The tax factor did not constitute an element entering into the decision to invest, and tax treaties had not the importance in this context with which they were often credited. The interests of the inward investor and the country of origin were not difficult to reconcile; the real problem arose from the taxation of world-wide income on the basis of subjective jurisdictional principles of domicile or residence. He was not against double tax treaties as such, and Latin American countries provided examples of their usefulness; but these treaties were not important in the final investment decision. The inward investor wanted safety and security; trust was more important than paper guarantees. So what were the advantages of a double tax treaty? For the developing country, the double tax treaty provided a more stable framework. It also provided the possibility of negotiating a tax sparing article, when this was practicable, which was not often enough.

The UN Model was the OECD Model with inadequate modifications, and the OECD Model itself was still in use between developed and developing countries. The OECD Model sought neutrality between different types of investment; but developing countries wanted non-neutrality in order to be able to attract investment from abroad. For developing countries all investment flows were one-way and not reciprocal. The Cartagena Agreement of the Andean Pact was more appropriate for developing countries than anything derived from the OECD Model, which taxed on the basis of the residence principle. The residence principle was inappropriate for developing countries; and yet it was noticeable that French and British ex-colonies in Africa followed French and British principles of treaty negotiation. Some very poor countries had adopted the residence principle which provided them with negligible tax revenue and was inappropriate to their circumstances. And little or no inward investment might be attracted to developing countries by tax treaties based on the residence principle.

Professor Muten agreed with *Mr. Figueroa* that taxes might not be a major determinant of the investment decision, and that in poor countries little tax revenue might be raised by the application of the residence principle. In developing countries the important principle was capital-import neutrality rather than capital-export neutrality. He invited Mr. Collins to speak.

Mr. Collins said that the interests of developing and industralised countries were not diametrically opposed. There were contrasts and differences within each group. The main purpose of tax treaties was to provide order instead of chaos. Each country decided for itself what its interests were and how these interests should be promoted. The advantages of tax treaties to taxpayers who were inward investors in developing countries were certainty, equity and assurance of freedom from arbitrary taxation and relief from international double taxation. The advantages for the government of the industrialised country were certainty, a firm basis of tax relief and the possibility of administrative assistance from the tax authorities in the developing country. The advantages of a double tax treaty for the government of a developing country were that it helped to promote inward investment and international trade, that it might provide for tax sparing, and that it offered the possibility of administrative assistance. Both industrialised and developing countries could choose what they put into a treaty and what they left out. In conclusion, *Mr. Collins* said that he could not agree with the proposition that double tax treaties were either always or never worthwhile.

Mr. Vaish posed the question whether double tax conventions were in the best interest of developing countries and whether capital-exporting countries were interested. He said that compliance with the taxes of another country could never be taken lightly. Double tax conventions made such compliance easier and enabled the taxpayer to determine his liability in advance with relative certainty. Unilateral double tax relief provisions, which were to be found in most capital-exporting tax jurisdictions, were often insufficient. Double tax conventions made life easier for the taxpayers of both countries. It had to be borne in mind that in the absence of a double tax treaty what was nominally a tax on the capital exporter was often in practice shifted to the business operating in the host country. Double tax treaties were thus of interest to both industrialised and developing countries, although the desire to negotiate a treaty would vary according to circumstances. In sum, treaties provided substantial advantages and these advantages generally outweighed the corresponding disadvantages. He thought it was generally worthwhile for a developing country to have a double tax treaty even with the United States.

Professor Mutén observed that India was a developed country by comparison with the least developed of the developing countries. This was also shown by the ample network of tax treaties that India had, both with industrial and less developed countries. He invited *Mr. Court* to speak.

Mr. Court said that it was difficult to generalise about treaties, because there were large differences between one treaty and another. The existence of a treaty was positive for relations between one developed country and another, both for the tax authorities and for businesses and their tax advisers. The OECD and UN Models were really flexible, and could be adapted to a variety of situations. As a matter of history, it should not be forgotten that double tax treaties had been developed by Europeans with underdeveloped, schedular systems of income taxation as was normal in developing countries. At the technical level, he did not believe that the UN Model was ill adapted to developing countries, but rather that the Models themselves (including the OECD Model) might not always be well adapted to modern transactions. He believed that taxation was an important influence on international investment decisions, and did not at all share the conclusion of some others that the UN Model was useless for the purpose of relieving international double taxation and thus removing an obstacle to international investment.

Mr. Feinberg said that treaties between developed countries had the same objectives as treaties between developed and developing countries, although it might be legitimate to question which country should bear the cost of granting relief from international double taxation. It was difficult to argue that taxation had no impact on international investment decisions at the margin, and it followed that double tax treaties must have a role to play. It might be legitimate for one country to decide that it would not be worth while to have a double tax treaty with some other country, although developing countries had made many requests to the United States for a double tax treay ty or at least for talks on the subject.

Professor Mutén opened the discussion of tax sparing by observing that it had been a subject at the IFA Montevideo Congress in 1968. He invited *Mr. Vaish* to speak.

Mr. Vaish said that India dit not enter into treaties for the relief of international double taxation unless they provided for tax sparing. The United States took the opposite line and refused to sign treaties if they provided for tax sparing. These were principled positions; in practice, something had to give if a treaty was to be signed at all. He disagreed with Mr. Feinberg's assertion that the form of capital export neutrality favoured by the United States promoted economic efficiency. Developing countries must have instruments to channel investment to where it was required; and tax incentives were among the most effective instruments for this purpose. It was important to have non-discrimination between resident and non-resident taxpayers, so that tax incentives would flow through to the investor and not be appropriated by the tax authorities in the investor's country of residence. The optimum size of an incentive to inward investment was a separate question. As *Mr. Feinberg* had pointed out, tax sparing could be limited or annihilated by tax credits, although tax sparing was a less important phenomenon at lower rates of tax.

Mr. Feinberg said that the United States was alone in the world on the subject of tax sparing, although he was not sure how important tax sparing was in practice. A matter of constitutional principle underlay the refusal to agree to tax sparing. It was US treaty policy that, with limited exceptions, US tax benefits were provided only to residents of a partner and not to US residents. It was the partner's concessions which benefited US persons; tax sparing credits would clearly violate this policy. This policy grew out of the US constitutional requirement that tax legislation originated in the House of Representatives, the Lower House, but only the Senate, the Upper House, had a role in the approval of treaties. Furthermore, within the Senate, the Foreign Relations Committee, and not the tax-writing Finance Committee, played the key role. This division of tax policy responsibilities among arms of the US legislature led to the decision many years ago that treaties could affect US taxation of foreign persons but US taxation of US persons would, as a general matter, remain a legislative responsibility. It had already been noted that US support for the concept of capital-export neutrality was based on considerations of economic efficiency. Moreover, it was objectionable to the United States that under a regime of tax sparing the level of benefit granted by the capital-exporting country to its investors depended, not on its own policies, but on the tax policies of the developing country. The broader the range of activities eligible for tax holidays in the developing country, the longer the holiday period and the higher the nominal tax rate in the developing country relatively to the effective rate under the tax holiday, the greater was the benefit. These features were solely under the control of the developing country. If the United States was to provide any tax benefits for investment in developing countries, it was argued that the scope of those benefits should be entirely within the control of the United States. He also disagreed with the argument that in the absence of tax sparing tax incentives were transferred dollar for dollar to the tax authorities in the capital-exporting country; there were a number of qualifications that mitigated the effect of this argument. To benefit from tax sparing the investor must repatriate profits.

By contrast, deferral of US tax without tax sparing encouraged the re-investment of profits. Re-investment, not repatriation, was what developing countries ought to be seeking. Moreover tax sparing encouraged countries with serious tax revenue problems to exacerbate their problems by granting tax holidays. Again, investors in a country with relatively low tax rates applied generally could not benefit from tax sparing, whereas investment in a country with a less efficient system of high tax rates and many tax holidays would stand to benefit if tax sparing were granted by the United States. If profits were immediately repatriated to the United States, tax-spared profits could be averaged with highly taxed profits; most multinational corporations had excess credits and tax sparing exacerbated this problem. Features of US law tended to mitigate the dollar for dollar offset effect of the foreign tax credit. The most important of these was deferral. A US investor was not normally subject to US tax on the earnings of a foreign subsidiary until those earnings were repatriated. Current US taxation of controlled foreign corporation profits under subpart F of the Internal Revenue Code generally did not apply to the kinds of investments which were eligible for developing country tax holidays. Thus, in the typical case, as long as tax holiday profits were not repatriated, there was no US tax and no offset to the tax holiday benefit. Deferral acted as an incentive to reinvest low-taxed profits. This was clearly in the development interest of the country of inward investment. In conclusion, he noted that the United States had some ten double tax treaties with developing countries in addition to three awaiting ratification.

Mr. Court said that tax sparing was widely used in French tax treaties, and experience was generally positive. However, given the recent decrease in the French rate of corporation tax and the level of taxation in a number of source countries, even with stepped tax sparing provisions, tax sparing clauses were often too powerful and thus gave rise to technical difficulties or even to schemes of tax reduction. A fair assessment was that tax sparing provisions were useful but should not be overplayed. In particular, their rates, which were often based on gross income, should be kept within a reasonsable range.

Mr. Figueroa said that it was essential that the tax sacrifice should be of real benefit to the host country; otherwise developing countries were pressed or forced into the adoption of soak-up taxes. Thus the grant of an incentive in the country of inward investment must be complemented by tax sparing. The US position was compatible with the OECD Model; but it was a 'take it or leave it' attitude, and the US was not bargaining on this point with treaty partners.

Mr. Collins said that since 1961 the UK had been prepared to include tax sparing provisions in an agreement with a developing country if this was consistent with producing a balance treaty overall; and more than thirty of the UK's agreements included such provisions. The legislation authorising their inclusion enabled the relief to be given only in relation to reliefs provided in the other country under legislation designed to promote industrial, commercial, scientific, educational or other development. Thus the UK had agreed to provide matching relief for tax spared in respect of clearly defined development projects which would patently help the partner country to strengthen its economic and industrial base. The UK had not provided matching relief for relief given under legislation specifically designed to promote exports, and it had never conceded 'across-the-board' matching credit for tax (such as withholding tax on dividends or interest) given up by the partner country under the terms of the agreement. In conclusion, he noted that the question of tax sparing had become less important than it used to be as a result of the reductions in rates of corporation tax both in the UK and elsewhere.

After the coffee break *Professor Mutén* opened the discussion of the concept of permanent establishment. He noted that developing countries generally wanted a broad definition of this term. He invited *Mr. Collins* to speak.

Mr. Collins said that the concept of permanent establishment was needed both to define the source of income and to measure the income originating in that source. Different tests could be applied, for example to an activity like marketing; but as the business expanded, eventually a permanent establishment would be required (unless its place was taken by a subsidiary). The presence or absence of a permanent establishment was related to the distinction in UK tax law between trading with and trading in. It was the function of the Models to provide criteria for determining the presence or absence of a permanent establishment. The concept of a permanent establishment was broader in the UN Model; but the functions were essentially the same in the Models of the UN and the OECD. The concept of a permanent establishment was a useful one, not least because its precise significance could be negotiated between the treaty partners; indeed, if there were no concept of a permanent establishment, an alternative would be required. In conclusion he noted that the significance and precise definition of a permanent establishment were changing as a result of the electronic revolution of recent years.

Professor Mutén said that Mr. Figueroa's predecessor on the UN group of experts had said that the adoption of the concept of a permanent establishment by this group was a manifestation of original sin. Some twenty years had been spent in looking for the truth and no consensus had been reached. The concept of a permanent establishment had originated in reciprocal or symmetrical relations between treaty partners. In Article 7 of the OECD Model the right to tax business profits was attributed exclusively to the investor's state of residence, except for profits originating in a permanent establishment in the other state; some people might feel that this formula had given rise to artificial schemes for avoiding business activities taking a form that would come under the definition of a permanent establishment. He invited Mr. Figueroa to speak.

Mr. Figueroa said that the OECD's 'effectively connected' principle was difficult and unsatisfactory. There were fewer conditions in some Latin American countries for the establishment of a taxing right. Despite a high level of activity in a developing country, payment for the eventual sale of the goods concerned might be made to the investor's country of residence. The concept of a permanent establishment was not easily compatible with the tax legislation of a number of developing countries, although a permanent establishment as modified by the 'force of attraction' principle might provide a basis for negotiation. The concept of a permanent establishment in the UN Model was a little better than in the OECD Model; but it was still not satisfactory.

Mr. Vaish said that the concept of a permanent establishment was not important in India except for banks. Indian tax officials in the field had difficulty with the concept of a permanent establishment, and were more familiar with the British concept of a 'business connection'.

Mr. Feinberg said that important differences between the OECD and UN Models were that the UN Model had a lower threshold of activity for a permanent establishment than the OECD, and that the UN Model levied tax at higher effective rates where tax was levied on the gross basis rather than the net. It was not correct that the United States had made no use of the UN Model in treaties with developing countries, as could be seen by studying a number of recent treaties. The United States attempted to compensate for the lack of tax sparing in its treaties with developing countries by a willingness to approach the topic of a permanent establishment flexibly and to lower the threshold of activity for a permanent establishment below what it would have found acceptable otherwise. He did not agree that the concept of a permanent establishment was useful only if there were reciprocal business relationships between the treaty partners. Even if there was no such reciprocity, it could be useful for both countries if a potential inward investor was able to explore the market, for example, without incurring the full tax liability attaching to a permanent establishment. But the concept of a permanent establishment could be useful to both countries (provided that only permanent-establishment-related income was subject to tax) because of the importance of the net basis of taxation: otherwise economic transactions and activities could easily be rendered uneconomic if tax were levied on the gross basis. The United States accepted only a limited 'force-of-attraction' principle, and then only under duress during the course of treaty negotiations.

Professor Mutén noted from the Panelists' papers that all their countries supported the principle of separate accounting as against unitary taxation. He moved the discussion to the exchange of information and asked *Mr. Vaish* to speak.

Mr. Vaish said that the information he would speak about was the expenses that distinguished the net basis of taxation from the gross. India has insisted on the gross basis of withholding tax on royalties, technical service fees, dividends and interests in all post-1976 tax treaties. In recent years more and more provisions had been introduced in India to tax non-residents on an assumed income basis. A foreign company engaged in civil construction or the erection of plant and machinery in connection with an approved turnkey power project was effectively taxed at 6.5 per cent of gross total payments received in respect of the project. There were similar provisions for tax on the business of the exploration of mineral oils, on shipping and on the operation of aircraft. Non-resident taxpayers were often content with this mode of taxation because it made the Indian tax liability certain, so that it could be built into the quotations for the work concerned. Even if the treaties did not incorporate this gross basis of taxation the taxpayer might opt for it on the basis provided in the statute if he thought that it would be more favourable to him than the usual basis of taxing the income of a permanent establishment. There were difficulties with the gross basis of taxation; in particular the rate of tax on expatriates working in India could be unbearably heavy, because the system was not designed to deal with this matter. He had reservations about the gross basis, which was not really income taxation at all; but the net basis could be very difficult to compute and agree with the tax authority. Finally, he noted that if the buyer and seller negotiated on the net basis, the seller was relieved of any obligation to gross up for tax and his price could be correspondingly keener.

Professor Mutén said that the exchange of information between tax authorities was a necessary evil to secure the advantages of the net basis of taxation.

Mr. Collins said that the gross basis was makeshift and expedient and not satisfactory in the long term. It did not give the right answer. It also aggravated the problems of correct tax computation in cases of transfer pricing.

Mr. Figueroa referred to the 38th IFA Congress in Buenos Aires in 1984, where Subject I had established that it was preferable to levy tax in the country of origin: taxation in the country of residence distorted and impeded the free flow of capital between countries.

Professor Mutén said that the United States had a number of tax information exchange agreements (TIEA's). These were double tax treaties for the exchange of information with no provision for relief from international double taxation. He asked *Mr. Feinberg* to speak.

Mr. Feinberg said that the United States entered into a tax information exchange agreement if it was proving impossible to negotiate a comprehensive income tax treaty. It was not generally appreciated that the benefits from the exchange of information could be reciprocal. However, the United States was concerned that it might be swamped by requests for information from developing countries; few requests for information from developing countries were made by the United States.

Miss Raitasuo, Finland, winner of the Mitchell B. Carroll Prize 1990, spoke of her work on tax sparing and associated tax credits. She had been drawn to this topic because it had seemed to her to be an unjustly neglected area. She had concerned herself with the theoretical framework of tax sparing, with United Nations work on this subject, with United States tax treaty policy towards tax sparing and with the application of tax sparing provisions by five developed countries - Canada, Finland, France, Germany, United Kingdom. Too much weight had been accorded to the admitted problems of tax neutrality, tax equity and the repatriation of profits, and the results in these five countries had not been encouraging. Most disappointing was the work of the United Nations because of their insistence un unanimity in policy towards tax sparing. It was ironical that this attitude was inconsistent with other provisions of the UN Model, which permitted the choice of the exemption method; the exemption method produced the same result as granting credits in the country of residence for tax spared in the country of origin. The UN experts had been distracted away from tax sparing into the different topic of assessing the effectiveness of tax incentives. She recognised that tax sparing provisions could be misused and doubted the effectiveness of what had been called 'sunset provisions', namely tax sparing arrangements with a limited life of five years or some similar period.

The discussion was opened to participants from the floor, and the following were the principal points made:

1.The presence or absence of a treaty was important to the investor from abroad. The investor was interested in a treaty with no overriding.

2. Exemption provided much the same results as tax sparing.

3.The article on permanent establishments was only a definitional article, and it was strange that the UN Model had made marginal activities constitute a permanent establishment. If this were to be justified, marginal activities should imply a marginal profit.

The Panel discussion resumed. *Mr. Feinberg* said that even if the permanent establishment generated no profits of its own, income might be attributed to it through the 'force-of-attraction' principle. The UN Model was useful at any rate as a starting point in negotiations between developed and developing countries. The UN groups of experts should seek to make tax administrators in developing countries more aware of the usefulness of exchanges of information and of the resolution of disputes through the competent authority procedure.

Mr. Figueroa said that the UN Model had stopped half-way; this must be corrected, and the reforms which the UN Model had started must be taken to their logical conclusion. The OECD Model also required reform in the same direction. These reforms might usefully be complemented by guarantees to investors from the host country government.

Mr. Collins said that unanimous agreement for change or even a wide consensus would be virtually unobtainable. It would be better to concentrate on refinements of the Model to meet existing criticisms.

Mr. Vaish said that the best topics of study for the UN group of experts would be the ways in which the treaties had worked, extended commentaries on the treaties, the training of tax administrators and refinements of the competent authority procedure.

Professor Mutén thanked the Panelists and participants from the floor and declared the Seminar closed.